gifts from the kitchen

Publications International, Ltd.

Favorite Brand Name Recipes at www.fbnr.com

Pictured on the front cover: Chocolate Peanut Butter Candy Bars *(page 59).*
Pictured on the back cover *(left to right):* Black Forest Banana Bread *(page 114)* and Ultimate White and Dark Chocolate Cookies *(page 29).*

ISBN-13: 978-1-4127-9790-0
ISBN-10: 1-4127-9790-X

Library of Congress Control Number: 2008943522

Manufactured in China.

8 7 6 5 4 3 2 1

Microwave Cooking: Microwave ovens vary in wattage. Use the cooking times as guidelines and check for doneness before adding more time.

Preparation/Cooking Times: Preparation times are based on the approximate amount of time required to assemble the recipe before cooking, baking, chilling or serving. These times include preparation steps such as measuring, chopping and mixing. The fact that some preparations and cooking can be done simultaneously is taken into account. Preparation of optional ingredients and serving suggestions is not included.

table of contents

cookie

Delights

cocoa crackles

1-1/2 cups all-purpose flour

1/3 cup unsweetened cocoa powder

1/2 teaspoon salt

1/2 teaspoon baking soda

1/2 cup (1 stick) butter, softened

1/2 cup granulated sugar

1/4 cup packed light brown sugar

2 eggs, lightly beaten

1 teaspoon vanilla

Powdered sugar

Makes about
3-1/2 dozen cookies

1. Preheat oven to 350°F. Lightly grease cookie sheets.

2. Combine flour, cocoa, salt and baking soda in medium bowl. Beat butter, granulated sugar and brown sugar in large bowl with electric mixer at medium speed until light and fluffy. Add eggs and vanilla; beat until well blended. Add flour mixture; beat just until blended.

3. Place powdered sugar in shallow bowl. Shape dough by heaping teaspoons into balls. Roll balls in powdered sugar; place 2 inches apart on prepared cookie sheets.

4. Bake about 11 minutes or until set and no longer shiny. Cool on cookie sheets 2 minutes. Remove to wire racks; cool completely.

poinsettia cookie bouquet

1 recipe Basic Gingerbread Dough (recipe follows)

1 recipe Royal Icing (recipe follows)

Burgundy food coloring

Coarse sugar or edible glitter

Assorted color dragées

Supplies

Flower-shaped cookie cutter or stencil

9 cookie sticks

Small icing spatula

Medium decorative container

Styrofoam rounds to fit container

Decorative straw

Makes about 9 cookies

1. Preheat oven to 350°F. Line cookie sheets with parchment paper.

2. Prepare Basic Gingerbread Dough. Roll warm dough to 1/2-inch thickness. Cut out poinsettias with cookie cutter. Re-roll dough scraps once to cut out more shapes. Place cookies 1 inch apart at opposite sides of cookie sheets, leaving middle of sheets empty. Press cookie sticks firmly into cookies, making sure sticks face middle of sheets. Bake 18 to 20 minutes or until firm and golden brown. Cool on cookie sheets 10 minutes. Transfer to wire racks; cool completely.

3. Prepare Royal Icing. Thin icing with water, if necessary. Tint icing very light burgundy. Transfer about 1/3 cup to small bowl; cover bowl. Tint remaining icing darker burgundy.

4. Spread thin layer dark burgundy icing with spatula just to edge of cookie. Immediately spoon about 1 teaspoon light burgundy icing in middle of cookie. Quickly drag toothpick through icing in middle to create a design. Place several dragées in middle. Sprinkle sugar on edges of cookie. Repeat with remaining cookies. Let dry completely.

5. Cut styrofoam to fit container. Stick cookies into styrofoam. Cover styrofoam with straw.

6. Serve cookies within 3 days. If cookies are intended for decoration only, they will keep for several weeks.

basic gingerbread dough

5 cups all-purpose flour

1 tablespoon ground ginger

2 teaspoons ground cinnamon

1 teaspoon salt

1 cup sugar

1 cup shortening

1 cup molasses

1. Sift together flour, ginger, cinnamon and salt in medium bowl; set aside.

2. Combine sugar, shortening and molasses in medium saucepan. Stir over low heat until shortening just melts. Pour into large mixing bowl. Let cool 5 minutes.

3. Add flour mixture to warm sugar mixture. Beat with electric mixer at low speed just until dough forms. Dough should be somewhat soft, but not sticky. Add more flour as needed. Let dough rest 5 minutes.

royal icing

4 egg whites*

4 cups powdered sugar, sifted

1 teaspoon almond extract or clear vanilla extract**

*Use only grade A clean, uncracked eggs.

**Icing remains very white when clear flavorings are used.

Beat egg whites in large bowl with electric mixer at high speed until foamy. Gradually add sugar and almond extract. Beat at high speed until thickened.

Note: When dry, Royal Icing is very hard and resistant to damage that can occur during shipping.

Makes 2 cups

chocolate chunk cookies

1-2/3 cups all-purpose flour

1/3 cup CREAM OF WHEAT® Hot Cereal (Instant, 1-minute, 2-1/2-minute or 10-minute cook time), uncooked

1/2 teaspoon baking soda

1/4 teaspoon salt

3/4 cup (1-1/2 sticks) butter, softened

1/2 cup packed brown sugar

1/3 cup granulated sugar

1 egg

1 teaspoon vanilla extract

1 (11.5-ounce) bag chocolate chunks

1 cup chopped pecans

1. Preheat oven to 375°F. Lightly grease cookie sheets. Blend flour, Cream of Wheat, baking soda and salt in medium bowl; set aside.

2. Beat butter and sugars in large bowl with electric mixer at medium speed until creamy. Add egg and vanilla. Beat until fluffy. Reduce speed to low. Add Cream of Wheat mixture; mix well. Stir in chocolate chunks and pecans.

3. Drop by tablespoonfuls onto prepared cookie sheets. Bake 9 to 11 minutes or until golden brown. Let stand on cookie sheets 1 minute before transferring to wire racks to cool completely.

Prep Time: 15 minutes

Start to Finish Time: 35 minutes

For a colorful item to give as a gift or take to school bake sales, replace the chocolate chunks with multicolored candy-coated chocolate.

Makes
24 cookies

cookie Delights

fortune cookies

Nonstick cooking spray

2 egg whites

1/3 cup all-purpose flour

1/3 cup sugar

1 tablespoon water

1/4 teaspoon vanilla

12 paper fortunes

1. Preheat oven to 400°F. Spray cookie sheet with cooking spray.

2. Whisk egg whites in small bowl until foamy. Add flour, sugar, water and vanilla; whisk until smooth.

3. Working in batches of 2, place 2 teaspoons batter on prepared cookie sheet. Spread batter evenly with back of spoon to 3-inch rounds. Spray with cooking spray. Bake 4 minutes or until edges are golden brown.

4. Working quickly, remove cookies from cookie sheet and invert onto work surface. Place fortune in centers. Fold cookies in half, pressing on seam. Fold in half again, pressing to hold together. Cool completely.

5. Repeat steps 3 and 4 with remaining batter.

Makes 1 dozen cookies

banana oatmeal caramel cookies

1 package (18 ounces) refrigerated turtle cookie dough

2 ripe bananas, mashed

1-1/3 cups uncooked old-fashioned oats

2/3 cup all-purpose flour

1/2 cup semisweet chocolate chips

Makes about 2 dozen cookies

1. Preheat oven to 350°F. Lightly grease cookie sheets. Let dough stand at room temperature about 15 minutes.

2. Beat dough, bananas, oats and flour in large bowl with electric mixer at medium speed until well blended. Drop dough by heaping tablespoonfuls 2 inches apart onto prepared cookie sheets; flatten slightly.

3. Bake 16 to 18 minutes or until edges are brown and centers are set. Cool on cookie sheets 1 minute. Remove to wire racks; cool completely.

4. Place chocolate chips in small resealable food storage bag. Microwave on MEDIUM (50%) 1 minute; knead bag lightly. Microwave and knead at additional 30-second intervals until chocolate is completely melted. Cut off tiny corner of bag. Drizzle melted chocolate over cookies. Let stand until set.

Variation: Use triple chocolate cookie dough instead of the turtle dough.

cookie Delights

toasted coconut pinwheels

1-1/4 cups sweetened flaked coconut

1 package (about 18 ounces) white cake mix

1 package (8 ounces) cream cheese, softened

1/4 cup all-purpose flour

1 teaspoon coconut extract or vanilla extract

3/4 cup apricot jam

1. Preheat oven to 350°F. Spread coconut on baking sheet; bake 4 minutes. Stir coconut and bake additional 4 minutes or until lightly browned. Set aside.

2. Beat cake mix, cream cheese, flour and coconut extract in large bowl with electric mixer at low speed until well blended. Place dough between 2 sheets parchment paper and roll into rectangle about 13×10 inches. Spread jam over dough, leaving 1/2-inch border. Sprinkle with toasted coconut.

3. Roll dough jelly-roll style starting from long side. (Do not roll paper up with dough.) Wrap in plastic wrap; freeze 2 hours or refrigerate 4 hours or overnight.

4. Preheat oven to 350°F. Spray cookie sheets with nonstick cooking spray.

5. Slice dough into 1/4-inch-thick slices; place 1 inch apart on prepared cookie sheets. Bake 12 to 15 minutes or until edges are just beginning to brown. Cool on cookie sheets 3 minutes. Remove to wire racks; cool completely.

Prep Time: 20 minutes

Chill Time: 2 to 4 hours

Bake Time: 15 minutes

Makes about
3 dozen cookies

carrot raisin spice cookies

1-1/4 cups all-purpose flour

1/2 cup CREAM OF WHEAT® Cereal (1-minute, 2-1/2-minute or 10-minute stovetop cooking)

1-1/2 teaspoons ground cinnamon

1 teaspoon pumpkin pie spice

3/4 teaspoon baking soda

1/2 cup (1 stick) margarine or butter, softened

1/2 cup granulated sugar

1/3 cup packed light brown sugar

1/4 cup egg substitute

1 teaspoon vanilla extract

1/2 cup finely grated carrot

1/2 cup seedless raisins

1/4 cup PLANTERS® Walnuts, finely chopped

Makes
2-1/2 dozen

cookie Delights

You may line the baking sheets with parchment paper as an alternative to greasing. It eliminates cleanup, bakes the cookies more evenly and allows them to cool right on the paper instead of on wire racks.

1. Mix flour, Cream of Wheat, cinnamon, pumpkin pie spice and baking soda in medium bowl; set aside.

2. Beat margarine or butter and sugars in large bowl with mixer until creamy; beat in egg substitute and vanilla.

3. Reduce speed to low; blend in flour mixture.

4. Stir in carrot, raisins and walnuts; let stand 10 minutes.

5. Drop by teaspoonfuls 2 inches apart onto lightly greased baking sheets.

6. Bake at 350°F for 10 to 12 minutes or until golden brown. Cool on wire racks.

snickerdoodles

3/4 cup plus 1 tablespoon sugar, divided

2 teaspoons ground cinnamon, divided

1-1/3 cups all-purpose flour

1 teaspoon cream of tartar

1/2 teaspoon baking soda

1/2 cup (1 stick) butter

1 egg

1 cup (6 ounces) cinnamon baking chips

1 cup raisins (optional)

Makes about 3 dozen cookies

1. Preheat oven to 400°F. Combine 1 tablespoon sugar and 1 teaspoon cinnamon in small bowl.

2. Combine flour, remaining 1 teaspoon cinnamon, cream of tartar and baking soda in medium bowl. Beat remaining 3/4 cup sugar and butter in large bowl with electric mixer at medium speed until creamy. Beat in egg. Gradually add flour mixture to sugar mixture, beating at low speed until stiff dough forms. Stir in cinnamon chips and raisins, if desired.

3. Roll dough into 1-inch balls; roll in cinnamon-sugar mixture. Place on ungreased cookie sheets.

4. Bake 10 minutes or until set. *Do not overbake.* Remove to wire racks; cool completely.

chocolate cherry gems

1 package (about 16 ounces) refrigerated sugar cookie dough

1/3 cup unsweetened Dutch process cocoa powder*

3 tablespoons maraschino cherry juice, divided

18 maraschino cherries, cut into halves

3/4 cup powdered sugar

*Dutch process, or European-style, cocoa gives these cookies an intense chocolate flavor and a dark, rich color. Unsweetened cocoa powder can be substituted, but the flavor may be milder and the color may be lighter.

1. Preheat oven to 350°F. Lightly grease cookie sheets. Let dough stand at room temperature about 15 minutes.

2. Beat dough, cocoa and 1 tablespoon cherry juice in large bowl with electric mixer at medium speed until well blended. Shape dough into 36 (3/4-inch) balls; place 2 inches apart on prepared cookie sheets. Flatten balls slightly; press cherry half into center of each ball.

3. Bake 9 to 11 minutes or until set. Cool on cookie sheets 2 minutes. Remove to wire racks; cool completely.

4. Combine powdered sugar and remaining 2 tablespoons cherry juice in small bowl; whisk until smooth. Add additional juice, 1 teaspoon at a time, if necessary, to create medium-thick pourable glaze. Drizzle glaze over cookies. Let stand until set.

Makes 3 dozen cookies

two-toned biscotti with pistachios and chocolate raisins

2/3 cup sugar

1/3 cup butter, softened

2 teaspoons baking powder

1/8 teaspoon salt

2 eggs

2 cups all-purpose flour

1/4 cup chopped pistachio nuts

2 tablespoons unsweetened cocoa powder

1/2 cup chocolate-covered raisins

1/4 teaspoon ground nutmeg

Makes about 2 dozen cookies

1. Preheat oven to 375°F. Lightly grease 2 cookie sheets.

2. Beat sugar and butter in large bowl with electric mixer at medium speed until light and fluffy. Add baking powder and salt; beat until well blended. Add eggs, 1 at a time, beating well after each addition. Gradually add flour, beating until well blended.

3. Divide dough in half. Stir nuts and cocoa into 1 portion of dough. Stir raisins and nutmeg into remaining dough. Divide each dough mixture in half.

4. Pat 1 portion chocolate dough into 8×6-inch rectangle. Shape 1 portion raisin dough into log; place in center of chocolate rectangle. Wrap chocolate dough around raisin log, flattening slightly. Place log on prepared cookie sheet, seam side down. Repeat with remaining dough.

5. Bake 40 to 50 minutes or until log sounds slightly hollow when tapped. Cool on cookie sheets 15 to 20 minutes or until warm but not hot. *Reduce oven temperature to 325°F.*

6. Cut each log diagonally into 3/4-inch slices with serrated knife. Place on ungreased cookie sheets. Bake 7 to 8 minutes. Turn slices; bake 7 to 8 minutes or until crisp.

lemon poppy thumbkins

2/3 cup (1-1/3 sticks) butter, softened

1/2 cup sugar

2 tablespoons grated lemon peel

2 egg yolks

1 teaspoon vanilla

1-1/2 cups all-purpose flour

1-1/2 teaspoons poppy seeds

1/4 teaspoon salt

1/4 cup prepared lemon curd

1. Beat butter in large bowl with electric mixer at medium speed 30 seconds. Add sugar and lemon peel; beat until just combined, about 30 seconds. Reduce mixer speed to low; beat in egg yolks and vanilla. Add flour, poppy seeds and salt all at once; beat until just combined. Cover with plastic wrap; refrigerate at least 1 hour or overnight.

2. Preheat oven 325°F. Line cookie sheets with parchment paper.

3. Scoop or shape dough into 24 balls. (Coat hands with nonstick cooking spray for easier handling.) Place balls 1 inch apart on prepared cookie sheets. Make deep indentation with thumb in each cookie. Bake 22 to 24 minutes or until just firm, but not brown. Cool on cookie sheets 2 minutes. Remove to wire racks; cool completely.

4. When ready to serve, fill center of each cookie with about 1/2 teaspoon lemon curd. Cookies are best served the same day as filled. Store covered in refrigerator.

Makes 2 dozen cookies

chocolate chip shortbread

1/2 cup (1 stick) butter, softened

1/2 cup sugar

1 teaspoon vanilla

1 cup all-purpose flour

1/4 teaspoon salt

1/2 cup mini semisweet chocolate chips

Makes 16 triangles

1. Preheat oven to 375°F.

2. Beat butter and sugar in large bowl with electric mixer at medium speed until light and fluffy. Beat in vanilla. Add flour and salt; beat at low speed until just combined. Stir in chocolate chips.

3. Divide dough in half. Press each half into ungreased 8-inch round cake pan.

4. Bake 12 minutes or until edges are golden brown. Score shortbread with knife (8 triangles per pan), taking care not to cut completely through shortbread.

5. Cool in pans on wire racks 10 minutes. Invert shortbread onto wire racks; cool completely. Break into triangles.

cocoa and peanut butter yummies

1-1/3 cups all-purpose flour

1/2 cup unsweetened cocoa powder

3/4 teaspoon baking soda

1/4 teaspoon salt

3/4 cup (1-1/2 sticks) butter, softened

1/2 cup granulated sugar

1/2 cup packed brown sugar

1 egg

2 tablespoons water

1/2 teaspoon vanilla

1 package (12 ounces) peanut butter chips

1. Preheat oven to 375°F. Combine flour, cocoa, baking soda and salt in medium bowl.

2. Beat butter, granulated sugar and brown sugar in large bowl with electric mixer at medium speed until smooth and creamy. Add egg, water and vanilla; beat 2 minutes. Add flour mixture; beat until well blended. Drop dough by rounded tablespoonfuls 3 inches apart onto ungreased cookie sheets.

3. Bake 8 to 10 minutes or until set. *Do not overbake.* Remove to wire racks; cool completely.

cookie *Delights*

Unsweetened cocoa powder is produced by grinding the dry substance remaining from the processed kernels, or nibs, of cocoa beans. It contains no additives.

Makes about
4 dozen cookies

tropical cookie balls

1 cup crushed coconut bar cookies (about 8 cookies)

1 bag (6 ounces) tropical medley dried fruit, finely minced*

1/4 teaspoon salt

1-1/2 cups finely chopped pecans, divided

1-1/2 cups shredded sweetened coconut, divided

1/2 teaspoon ground cinnamon

1/3 cup light corn syrup

2 tablespoons honey

1 teaspoon rum extract

*Or substitute 1 cup of minced dried fruits, such as mango, pineapple, golden or dark raisins and papaya.

1. Combine cookie crumbs, dried fruit and salt in large bowl; stir well. Add 1 cup pecans, 1/2 cup coconut and cinnamon; mix well.

2. Stir in corn syrup, honey and rum extract. Knead by hand until mixture comes together. Shape into 1-inch balls.

3. Combine remaining 1/2 cup pecans and 1 cup coconut in medium bowl. Roll balls in mixture to coat.

Makes about 3 dozen

cookie Delights

mocha cookie balls

1-3/4 cups chocolate graham cracker crumbs (9 to 11 crackers)

1-1/2 cups (8 ounces) chocolate-covered coffee beans, coarsely chopped

1 cup finely chopped walnuts

1 teaspoon instant coffee powder (optional)

1/4 teaspoon salt

3/4 cup dark corn syrup

1 teaspoon vanilla

1/2 cup powdered sugar

Makes about 4 dozen

1. Combine graham cracker crumbs, coffee beans, walnuts, coffee powder, if desired, and salt in large bowl; stir well.

2. Stir in corn syrup and vanilla. Knead by hand until mixture comes together. Shape into 1-inch balls.

3. Spread powdered sugar on baking sheet; roll balls in sugar to coat.

Variation: Roll the balls in unsweetened cocoa powder. Or, omit the chocolate-covered coffee beans and instant coffee powder; substitute 1-1/2 cups coarsely chopped bite-size chocolate-covered toffee pieces.

3-d holiday cookies

1/2 cup (1 stick) butter, softened

1/3 cup granulated sugar

2 tablespoons firmly packed light brown sugar

1 large egg

1/2 teaspoon vanilla extract

1-1/2 cups all-purpose flour

1/2 teaspoon baking powder

1/8 teaspoon salt

Decorating Glaze (recipe follows)

Assorted food colorings

1/2 cup "M&M's"® Chocolate Mini Baking Bits

Makes 18 (3-d) cookies

In large bowl cream butter and sugars until light and fluffy; beat in egg and vanilla. In small bowl combine flour, baking powder and salt; blend into creamed mixture. Wrap and refrigerate dough 2 to 3 hours. Preheat oven to 375°F. Working with half of dough at a time on lightly floured surface, roll to 1/8-inch thickness. Cut into pairs of desired shapes using 3-inch cookie cutters. Reroll trimmings and cut out more pairs. Place cutouts 1 inch apart on ungreased cookie sheets. Bake 5 to 7 minutes. Immediately cut 1 cookie of each pair in half vertically. Cool on cookie sheets 1 minute; cool completely on wire racks. Prepare Decorating Glaze. Tint glaze with food colorings as desired. Spread line of glaze down cut edge of half cookie. Press half cookie to middle of whole cookie; let set. Repeat with remaining half cookie, attaching half cookie to middle back of whole cookie. Spread glaze over entire 3-D cookies; let set. Using glaze to attach, decorate cookies with "M&M's"® Chocolate Mini Baking Bits. Store in tightly covered container.

Decorating Glaze: In large bowl combine 4 cups powdered sugar and 1/4 cup water until smooth. If necessary, add additional water, 1 teaspoon at a time, to make a medium-thick pourable glaze.

cookie Delights

ultimate white and dark chocolate cookies

2-1/3 cups all-purpose flour

1 teaspoon baking soda

1/4 teaspoon salt

1 cup (2 sticks) butter, softened

3/4 cup granulated sugar

3/4 cup packed brown sugar

2 eggs

2 tablespoons almond-flavored liqueur

1 teaspoon vanilla

1-1/2 cups white chocolate chips

1-1/2 cups bittersweet or semisweet chocolate chips

1 cup coarsely chopped pecans

Makes about 5 dozen cookies

1. Preheat oven to 375°F. Combine flour, baking soda and salt in medium bowl.

2. Beat butter, granulated sugar and brown sugar in large bowl with electric mixer until smooth and creamy. Beat in eggs, liqueur and vanilla. Add flour mixture; beat until well blended. Stir in chocolate chips and pecans. Drop dough by rounded teaspoonfuls 2 inches apart onto ungreased cookie sheets.

3. Bake 8 to 10 minutes or until set. *Do not overbake.* Remove to wire racks; cool completely.

irresistible

Snacks

party mix

3 cups bite-size rice cereal squares

2 cups toasted oat ring cereal

2 cups bite-size wheat cereal squares

1 cup pistachio nuts or peanuts

1 cup thin pretzel sticks

1/2 cup (1 stick) butter, melted

1 tablespoon Worcestershire sauce

1 teaspoon seasoned salt

1/2 teaspoon garlic powder

1/8 teaspoon ground red pepper (optional)

Makes 10 cups

Slow Cooker Directions

1. Combine cereals, nuts and pretzels in slow cooker.

2. Mix butter, Worcestershire sauce, seasoned salt, garlic powder and red pepper, if desired, in small bowl. Pour over cereal mixture in slow cooker; toss lightly to coat.

3. Cover; cook on LOW 3 hours, stirring well every 30 minutes. Cook, uncovered, 30 minutes more. Store cooled party mix in airtight container.

chili cashews

1 tablespoon vegetable oil

2 teaspoons chili powder

1 teaspoon ground cumin

1/2 teaspoon sugar

1/2 teaspoon red pepper flakes

2 cups roasted salted whole cashews (about 9 ounces)

Makes
1 (1-pint) jar

1. Preheat oven to 350°F. Line baking sheet with foil. Spray foil with nonstick cooking spray.

2. Combine oil, chili powder, cumin, sugar and red pepper flakes in medium bowl; stir until well blended. Add cashews, stirring to coat evenly. Spread mixture in single layer on prepared baking sheet. Bake 8 to 10 minutes or until golden, stirring once.

3. Cool completely on baking sheet. Transfer cashews to 1-pint wide-mouth jar. Seal jar.

4. Decorate jar and attach gift tag/recipe card.

Serving Suggestions: Try Chili Cashews as a snack or an appetizer. Or sprinkle it on salads or cottage cheese for a zesty treat.

cranberry gorp

1/4 cup (1/2 stick) butter

1/4 cup packed light brown sugar

1 tablespoon maple syrup

1 teaspoon curry powder

1/2 teaspoon ground cinnamon

1-1/2 cups dried cranberries

1-1/2 cups coarsely chopped walnuts and/or slivered almonds

1-1/2 cups lightly salted pretzel nuggets

Makes 20 servings

1. Preheat oven to 300°F. Grease 15×10-inch jelly-roll pan. Combine butter, brown sugar and maple syrup in large saucepan; heat over medium heat until butter is melted. Stir in curry powder and cinnamon. Add cranberries, walnuts and pretzels; stir until well blended.

2. Spread mixture on prepared pan. Bake 15 minutes or until mixture is crunchy and light brown.

green's "easier than pie" pretzel sticks

1 cup "M&M's"® Chocolate Mini Baking Bits
4 squares (1 ounce each) semi-sweet chocolate, divided
12 pretzel rods, divided
4 squares (1 ounce each) white chocolate, divided

Makes 12 pretzel sticks

Line baking sheet with waxed paper; set aside. Place "M&M's"® Chocolate Mini Baking Bits in shallow dish; set aside. In top of double boiler over hot water melt 3 squares semi-sweet chocolate. Remove from heat. Dip 6 pretzel rods into chocolate, spooning chocolate to coat about 3/4 of each pretzel. Press into and sprinkle with "M&M's"® Chocolate Mini Baking Bits; place on prepared baking sheet. Refrigerate until chocolate is firm. In top of double boiler over hot water melt 3 squares white chocolate. Remove from heat. Dip remaining 6 pretzel rods into chocolate, spooning chocolate to coat about 3/4 of each pretzel. Press into and sprinkle with "M&M's"® Chocolate Mini Baking Bits; place on prepared baking sheet. Refrigerate until chocolate is firm. Place remaining 1 square semi-sweet chocolate in small microwave-safe bowl; place remaining 1 square white chocolate in separate small microwave-safe bowl. Microwave at HIGH 30 seconds; stir. Repeat as necessary until chocolates are completely melted, stirring at 10-second intervals. Drizzle white chocolate over semi-sweet chocolate-dipped pretzels; drizzle semi-sweet chocolate over white chocolate-dipped pretzels. Sprinkle pretzels with any remaining "M&M's"® Chocolate Mini Baking Bits. Refrigerate 10 minutes or until firm. Store tightly covered at room temperature.

crunchy-fruity snack mix

1 cup (4 ounces) roasted and salted soy nuts

1 cup broken-in-half pretzel sticks (about 1-1/2 ounces)

2/3 cup dried cranberries

2/3 cup dried pineapple, cut into 1/2-inch pieces

2/3 cup white chocolate chips

1. Combine all ingredients in large bowl. Transfer mixture to 1-quart wide-mouth jar. Seal jar.

2. Decorate jar and attach gift tag/recipe card.

Serving Suggestions: Try Crunchy-Fruity Snack Mix on hot or cold cereal for breakfast, sprinkle it on waffles or pancakes, or use it as an ice cream topper. Also try it mixed into muffin, quick bread or cookie doughs or batters.

Makes
1 (1-quart) jar

apples 'n cinnamon popcorn

1 package plain microwave popcorn

1/4 cup (1/2 stick) butter, melted

1 packet CREAM OF WHEAT® Apples 'n Cinnamon Instant Hot Cereal, uncooked

Microwave popcorn as directed on package. Carefully open bag and pour popcorn into large bowl. Drizzle on butter and toss to coat evenly. Sprinkle Cream of Wheat over popcorn and toss to coat evenly.

Tip: For a fun treat, serve with slices of apple. And for additional variety, toss the popcorn with another Cream of Wheat flavor.

Prep Time: 5 minutes

Start to Finish Time: 10 minutes

Makes
6 servings

irresistible *Snacks*

honey popcorn clusters

Vegetable cooking spray

6 cups air-popped popcorn

2/3 cup DOLE® Golden or Seedless Raisins

1/2 cup DOLE® Chopped Dates or Pitted Dates, chopped

1/3 cup almonds (optional)

1/3 cup packed brown sugar

1/4 cup honey

2 tablespoons margarine

1/4 teaspoon baking soda

Makes 7 cups

- Line bottom and sides of 13×9-inch baking pan with large sheet of aluminum foil. Spray foil with vegetable cooking spray.

- Stir together popcorn, raisins, dates and almonds in foil-lined pan.

- Combine brown sugar, honey and margarine in small saucepan. Bring to boil over medium heat, stirring constantly; reduce heat to low. Cook 5 minutes. Do not stir. Remove from heat.

- Stir in baking soda. Pour evenly over popcorn mixture, stirring quickly to coat mixture evenly.

- Bake at 300°F 12 to 15 minutes or until mixture is lightly browned, stirring once halfway through baking time.

- Lift foil from pan; place on cooling rack. Cool popcorn mixture completely; break into clusters. Popcorn can be stored in airtight container up to 1 week.

Prep Time: 20 minutes

Bake Time: 15 minutes

nutty ginger snack mix

1/2 cup (about 2-1/2 ounces) finely diced crystallized ginger

1/2 cup (about 2-1/2 ounces) toasted pine nuts

1/2 cup (about 2 ounces) roasted salted pepitas or pumpkin seeds

1/2 cup toasted unsalted slivered almonds (about 2 ounces)

1. Combine all ingredients in large bowl. Transfer mixture to 1-pint wide-mouth jar. Seal jar.

2. Decorate jar and attach gift tag/recipe card.

Makes
1 (1-pint) jar

curried snack mix

3 tablespoons butter

2 tablespoons packed light brown sugar

1-1/2 teaspoons hot curry powder

1/4 teaspoon salt

1/4 teaspoon ground cumin

2 cups rice cereal squares

1 cup walnut halves

1 cup dried cranberries

Makes 16 servings

Slow Cooker Directions

1. Melt butter in large skillet. Add brown sugar, curry powder, salt and cumin; mix well. Add cereal, walnuts and cranberries; stir to coat. Transfer mixture to slow cooker.

2. Cover; cook on LOW 3 hours. Remove cover; cook 30 minutes.

quick and easy caramel corn

PAM® Original No-Stick Cooking Spray

1 bag (3.3 ounces) Orville Redenbacher's® Gourmet® Butter Microwave Popcorn

1/2 cup Fleischmann's® Original Margarine-stick (1/2 cup = 1 stick)

1 cup firmly packed light brown sugar

1/4 cup light corn syrup

1/4 teaspoon kosher salt

1/2 teaspoon baking soda

Makes
8 servings

1. Preheat oven to 300°F. Lightly spray 15×10-inch shallow baking pan with cooking spray; set aside. Spray large bowl with cooking spray; set aside.

2. Prepare popcorn according to package directions. Remove all unpopped kernels. Place popped corn in bowl.

3. Place Fleischmann's, brown sugar, corn syrup and salt in medium saucepan. Heat over medium heat until Fleischmann's melts, stirring well to combine. Cook WITHOUT STIRRING until candy thermometer reaches soft-ball stage (235°F to 240°F), about 10 minutes.

4. Remove brown sugar mixture from heat. Stir in baking soda until well blended. Quickly drizzle caramel over popped corn. Using two spatulas, carefully toss to coat evenly. Spread in single layer in pan.

5. Bake 15 minutes, stirring every 5 minutes to distribute caramel evenly. Remove from oven and stir again. Cool completely on waxed paper. Serve or store in tightly sealed container.

Cook's Tips: To remove unpopped kernels easily, place popped corn in large bowl. Gently lift and transfer popped corn to another bowl with one's hands. Add a handful of your favorite nuts to this recipe. If making a larger batch, place caramel coated popcorn in large aluminum roaster for easier stirring while baking.

Hands On Time: 30 minutes

Total Time: 30 minutes

bite-you-back roasted edamame

2 teaspoons vegetable oil

2 teaspoons honey

1/4 teaspoon wasabi powder*

1 package (10 ounces) shelled
   edamame, thawed if frozen

Kosher salt

*Available in the Asian section of most supermarkets
and in Asian specialty markets.*

Makes
4 servings

1. Preheat oven to 375°F.

2. Combine oil, honey and wasabi powder in large bowl; mix well. Add edamame; toss to coat.
Spread on baking sheet in single layer.

3. Bake 12 to 15 minutes or until golden brown, stirring once. Immediately remove from baking
sheet; sprinkle generously with salt. Cool completely before serving. Store in airtight container.

rosemary-scented nut mix

Makes 32 servings

2 tablespoons unsalted butter

2 cups pecan halves

1 cup unsalted macadamia nuts

1 cup walnuts

1 teaspoon dried rosemary

1/2 teaspoon salt

1/4 teaspoon red pepper flakes

1. Preheat oven to 300°F. Melt butter in large saucepan over low heat. Add pecans, macadamia nuts and walnuts; mix well. Add rosemary, salt and red pepper flakes; cook and stir about 1 minute.

2. Spread mixture onto ungreased nonstick baking sheet. Bake 15 minutes, stirring occasionally. Cool completely on baking sheet on wire rack.

super flavor-blasted party snack mix

2 cups PEPPERIDGE FARM® Flavor Blasted
   Goldfish® Snacks, any variety

2 cups PEPPERIDGE FARM® Baby Goldfish® Baked
   Snack Crackers

2 cups PEPPERIDGE FARM® Pretzel Goldfish® Baked
   Snack Crackers

1/2 cup dried cranberries

1/2 cup semi-sweet chocolate chips

1/2 cup mini marshmallows

1. Toss together all ingredients. Store in airtight container in cool, dry place.

Prep Time: 10 minutes

Makes
7-1/2 cups

drizzled party popcorn

8 cups popped popcorn

1/2 cup HERSHEY'S Milk Chocolate Chips

1/2 cup REESE'S® Peanut Butter Chips

2 teaspoons shortening (do not use butter, margarine, spread or oil)

1. Line cookie sheet or jelly-roll pan with waxed paper. Spread popcorn in thin layer on prepared pan.

2. Place milk chocolate chips and 1 teaspoon shortening in microwave-safe bowl. Microwave at MEDIUM (50%) 1 minute; stir. If necessary, microwave at MEDIUM an additional 15 seconds at a time, stirring after each heating, until chips are melted and smooth when stirred. Drizzle over popcorn.

3. Place peanut butter chips and remaining 1 teaspoon shortening in separate microwave-safe bowl. Microwave at MEDIUM 1 minute; stir. If necessary, microwave at MEDIUM an additional 15 seconds at a time, stirring after each heating, until chips are melted and smooth when stirred. Drizzle over popcorn.

4. Allow drizzle to set up at room temperature or refrigerate about 10 minutes or until firm. Break popcorn into pieces.

Popcorn is best eaten the same day as prepared, but it can be stored in an airtight container. Recipe amounts can be changed to match your personal preferences.

Makes about
8 cups popcorn

irresistible Snacks

parmesan ranch snack mix

3 cups corn or rice cereal squares

2 cups oyster crackers

1 package (5 ounces) bagel chips, broken in half

1-1/2 cups mini pretzel twists

1 cup shelled pistachio nuts

2 tablespoons grated Parmesan cheese

1/4 cup (1/2 stick) butter, melted

1 package (1 ounce) dry ranch salad dressing mix

1/2 teaspoon garlic powder

Slow Cooker Directions

1. Combine cereal, oyster crackers, bagel chips, pretzels, nuts and Parmesan cheese in slow cooker; mix gently.

2. Combine butter, salad dressing mix and garlic powder in small bowl. Pour over cereal mixture; toss lightly to coat. Cover; cook on LOW 3 hours.

3. Remove cover; stir gently. Cook, uncovered, 30 minutes.

Prep Time: 5 minutes
Cook Time: 3-1/2 hours

Makes
about 9-1/2 cups

chipotle-spiced nuts

1 pound mixed nuts

4 tablespoons butter, melted

2 tablespoons ORTEGA® Chipotle Taco Seasoning Mix

1 tablespoon light brown sugar

Preheat oven to 325°F. Toss nuts, butter, seasoning mix and brown sugar in large bowl until well combined.

Spread nut mixture on baking pan. Bake 20 minutes, stirring after 10 minutes. Serve warm, if desired. To store, allow to cool, and place in airtight container for up to 2 weeks.

Serving Suggestion: Try sprinkling these nuts over your favorite ice cream for a flavorful "hot" and cold dessert.

Tip: For gift-giving to friends and family, pack these deliciously spicy nuts in a decorative tin can. You can share the recipe on a gift tag, too!

Prep Time: 5 minutes

Start to Finish: 25 minutes

Makes 1 pound

popcorn granola

1 cup uncooked quick oats

6 cups air-popped popcorn

1 cup golden raisins

1/2 cup (2 ounces) chopped mixed dried fruit

1/4 cup (1 ounce) sunflower kernels

2 tablespoons butter

2 tablespoons packed light brown sugar

1 tablespoon honey

1/4 teaspoon ground cinnamon

1/4 teaspoon ground nutmeg

1. Preheat oven to 350°F. Spread oats on ungreased baking sheet; bake 10 to 15 minutes or until lightly toasted, stirring occasionally.

2. Combine oats, popcorn, raisins, dried fruit and sunflower kernels in large bowl. Heat butter, sugar, honey, cinnamon and nutmeg in small saucepan over medium heat until butter is melted. Drizzle over popcorn mixture; toss to coat.

Makes
8 servings

sweet & spicy beer nuts

2 cups pecan halves

2 teaspoons salt

2 teaspoons chili powder

2 teaspoons olive oil

1/2 teaspoon ground cumin

1/4 teaspoon ground red pepper

1/2 cup sugar

1/2 cup beer

1. Preheat oven to 350°F. Line baking sheet with foil.

2. Mix pecans, salt, chili powder, olive oil, cumin and red pepper in small bowl. Spread on prepared baking sheet. Toast 10 minutes or until fragrant. Cool on baking sheet on wire rack.

3. Combine sugar and beer in small saucepan. Heat over medium-high heat until mixture registers 250°F on candy thermometer. Remove from heat; carefully stir in nuts and any loose spices. Spread sugared nuts on foil-lined baking sheet, separating clusters.

4. Let cool completely. Break up any large pieces before serving.

Makes 3 cups

irresistible *Snacks*

cinnamon caramel corn

8 cups air-popped popcorn (about 1/3 cup kernels)

2 tablespoons honey

4 teaspoons butter

1/4 teaspoon ground cinnamon

Makes 4 servings

1. Preheat oven to 350°F. Spray jelly-roll pan with nonstick cooking spray. Place popcorn in large bowl.

2. Cook and stir honey, butter and cinnamon in small saucepan over low heat until butter is melted and mixture is smooth. Immediately pour over popcorn; toss to coat evenly. Pour onto prepared pan. Bake 12 to 14 minutes or until coating is golden brown and appears crackled, stirring twice.

3. Let cool on pan 5 minutes. (As popcorn cools, coating becomes crisp. If not crisp enough, or if popcorn softens upon standing, return to oven and heat 5 to 8 minutes.)

Cajun Popcorn: Preheat oven and prepare jelly-roll pan as directed above. Combine 7 teaspoons honey, 4 teaspoons butter and 1 teaspoon Cajun or Creole seasoning in small saucepan. Proceed with recipe as directed above.

Italian Popcorn: Spray 8 cups air-popped popcorn with butter-flavored cooking spray to coat. Sprinkle with 2 tablespoons grated Parmesan cheese, 1/2 teaspoon dried oregano and 1/8 teaspoon black pepper. Gently toss to coat.

brownies

and Bars

raspberry almond squares

1 package (about 18 ounces) yellow cake mix

1/2 cup sliced almonds, coarsely chopped

1/2 cup (1 stick) butter, melted

1 jar (12 ounces) seedless raspberry jam

1 package (8 ounces) cream cheese, softened

2 tablespoons all-purpose flour

1 egg

1. Preheat oven to 350°F. Line 13×9-inch baking pan with foil.

2. Beat cake mix, almonds and butter in large bowl with electric mixer at medium speed until crumbly. Reserve 1 cup mixture; press remaining mixture into bottom of prepared pan. Bake 10 to 12 minutes or until light golden brown.

3. Spread jam evenly over crust. Beat cream cheese, flour and egg in medium bowl at medium speed until combined. Spread gently over jam; top with reserved crumb mixture.

4. Bake 18 to 20 minutes or until light golden brown. Cool completely in pan on wire rack.

Tip: When lining pan with foil, allow 2 inches to hang over each end. Once the squares cool, you will be able to lift them out with ease.

Prep Time: 10 minutes

Bake Time: 28 to 32 minutes

triple layer chocolate bars

1-1/2 cups graham cracker crumbs

1/2 cup HERSHEY'S Cocoa, divided

1/4 cup sugar

1/2 cup (1 stick) butter or margarine, melted

1 can (14 ounces) sweetened condensed milk (not evaporated milk)

1/4 cup all-purpose flour

1 egg

1 teaspoon vanilla extract

1/2 teaspoon baking powder

3/4 cup chopped nuts

2 cups (12-ounce package) HERSHEY'S SPECIAL DARK® Chocolate Chips or HERSHEY'S Semi-Sweet Chocolate Chips

Makes 24 to 36 bars

1. Heat oven to 350°F. Stir graham cracker crumbs, 1/4 cup cocoa and sugar in medium bowl; stir in butter, blending well. Press mixture firmly onto bottom of ungreased 13×9×2-inch baking pan.

2. Beat sweetened condensed milk, flour, egg, vanilla, baking powder and remaining 1/4 cup cocoa in small bowl. Stir in nuts. Spread evenly over prepared crust. Sprinkle chocolate chips over top.

3. Bake 25 minutes or until set. Cool completely in pan on wire rack. Cut into bars. Store tightly covered at room temperature.

chocolate peanut butter candy bars

1 package (about 18 ounces) devil's food or dark chocolate cake mix without pudding in the mix

1 can (5 ounces) evaporated milk

1/3 cup butter, melted

1/2 cup dry-roasted peanuts

4 packages (1-1/2 ounces each) chocolate peanut butter cups, coarsely chopped

Makes about 2 dozen bars

1. Preheat oven to 350°F. Lightly grease 13×9-inch baking pan.

2. Beat cake mix, evaporated milk and butter in large bowl with electric mixer at medium speed until well blended. (Dough will be stiff.) Spread two thirds of dough in prepared pan. Sprinkle with peanuts.

3. Bake 10 minutes. Sprinkle with chopped candy. Drop remaining dough by large tablespoonfuls over candy.

4. Bake 15 to 20 minutes or until center is firm to the touch. Cool completely in pan on wire rack.

layers of love chocolate brownies

3/4 cup all-purpose flour

3/4 cup NESTLÉ® TOLL HOUSE® Baking Cocoa

1/4 teaspoon salt

1/2 cup (1 stick) butter, cut into pieces

1/2 cup granulated sugar

1/2 cup packed brown sugar

3 large eggs, divided

2 teaspoons vanilla extract

1 cup chopped pecans

3/4 cup NESTLÉ® TOLL HOUSE® Premier White Morsels

1/2 cup caramel ice cream topping

3/4 cup NESTLÉ® TOLL HOUSE® Semi-Sweet Chocolate Morsels

Makes
16 brownies

PREHEAT oven to 350°F. Grease 8-inch square baking pan.

COMBINE flour, cocoa and salt in small bowl. Beat butter, granulated sugar and brown sugar in large mixer bowl until creamy. Add 2 eggs, one at a time, beating well after each addition. Add vanilla extract; mix well. Gradually beat in flour mixture. Reserve 3/4 cup batter. Spread remaining batter into prepared baking pan. Sprinkle pecans and white morsels over batter. Drizzle caramel topping over top. Beat remaining egg and reserved batter in same large bowl until light in color. Stir in semi-sweet morsels. Spread evenly over caramel topping.

BAKE for 30 to 35 minutes or until center is set. Cool completely in pan on wire rack. Cut into squares.

coffee brownie bites

1 package (21 ounces) fudge brownie mix

3 eggs

1/2 cup vegetable oil

2 teaspoons instant coffee granules

2 teaspoons coffee liqueur (optional)

Powdered sugar (optional)

1. Preheat oven 325°F. Lightly spray 48 mini (1-3/4-inch) muffin cups with nonstick cooking spray.

2. Combine brownie mix, eggs, oil, coffee granules and coffee liqueur, if desired, in medium bowl. Mix according to package directions.

3. Fill each cup with 1 tablespoon brownie mixture. Bake 13 to 14 minutes or until toothpick inserted into centers comes out almost clean.

4. Transfer brownies to wire rack; cool completely. Sprinkle with powdered sugar. Store in airtight container.

Makes 4 dozen brownies

chocolate chunk oat bars

1 cup all-purpose flour

1/2 teaspoon baking soda

1/2 teaspoon salt

1 cup packed light brown sugar

1/2 cup (1 stick) butter, softened

1 egg

1 tablespoon water

1 teaspoon vanilla

1-1/2 cups uncooked old-fashioned oats

2 cups semisweet chocolate chunks, divided

Makes about 2 dozen bars

1. Preheat oven to 375°F. Lightly grease 9-inch square baking pan. Combine flour, baking soda and salt in small bowl.

2. Beat brown sugar and butter in large bowl with electric mixer at medium-high speed until creamy. Add egg, water and vanilla; beat until well blended. Stir in flour mixture and oats; mix well. Stir in 1-1/2 cups chocolate chunks.

3. Spread dough evenly in prepared pan; sprinkle with remaining 1/2 cup chocolate chunks. Bake about 30 minutes or just until center feels firm. Cool completely in pan on wire rack.

easy turtle bars

1 package (about 18 ounces) chocolate cake mix

1/2 cup (1 stick) butter, melted

1/4 cup milk

1 cup (6 ounces) semisweet chocolate chips

1 cup chopped pecans, divided

1 jar (12 ounces) caramel ice cream topping

1. Preheat oven to 350°F. Spray 13×9-inch baking pan with nonstick cooking spray.

2. Combine cake mix, butter and milk in large bowl; stir until well blended. Spread half of mixture into prepared pan.

3. Bake 7 to 8 minutes or until crust begins to form. Sprinkle chocolate chips and half of pecans over crust. Drizzle with caramel topping. Drop spoonfuls of remaining batter over caramel; sprinkle with remaining pecans.

4. Bake 18 to 20 minutes or until top springs back when lightly touched. (Caramel center will be soft.) Cool completely in pan on wire rack.

Makes
2-1/2 dozen bars

perfectly peppermint brownies

3/4 cup HERSHEY'S Cocoa

1/2 teaspoon baking soda

2/3 cup (1-1/3 sticks) butter or margarine, melted and divided

1/2 cup boiling water

2 cups sugar

2 eggs

1-1/3 cups all-purpose flour

1 teaspoon vanilla extract

1/4 teaspoon salt

1-1/3 cups (8-ounce package) YORK® Mini Peppermint Patties*

*You may substitute 16 to 17 small (1-1/2-inch) YORK Peppermint Patties, unwrapped and coarsely chopped, for the mini peppermint patties.

> Makes about 3 dozen brownies

1. Heat oven to 350°F. Grease 13×9×2-inch baking pan.

2. Stir together cocoa and baking soda in large bowl; stir in 1/3 cup butter. Add boiling water; stir until mixture thickens. Stir in sugar, eggs and remaining 1/3 cup butter; stir until smooth. Add flour, vanilla and salt; blend completely. Stir in peppermint patties. Spread in prepared pan.

3. Bake 35 to 40 minutes or until brownies begin to pull away from sides of pan. Cool completely in pan on wire rack. Cut into bars.

peanutty cranberry bars

1/2 cup (1 stick) butter or margarine, softened

1/2 cup granulated sugar

1/4 cup packed light brown sugar

1 cup all-purpose flour

1 cup quick-cooking rolled oats

1/4 teaspoon baking soda

1/4 teaspoon salt

1 cup REESE'S® Peanut Butter Chips

1-1/2 cups fresh or frozen whole cranberries

2/3 cup light corn syrup

1/2 cup water

1 teaspoon vanilla extract

Makes about 16 bars

Always use the pan size called for in the recipe. Substituting a different pan will affect the bars' texture. A smaller pan will give the bars a more cakelike texture; a larger pan will produce a flatter bar with a drier texture.

1. Heat oven to 350°F. Grease 8-inch square baking pan.

2. Beat butter, granulated sugar and brown sugar in medium bowl until fluffy. Stir together flour, oats, baking soda and salt; gradually add to butter mixture, mixing until mixture is consistency of coarse crumbs. Stir in peanut butter chips.

3. Reserve 1-1/2 cups mixture for crumb topping. Firmly press remaining mixture evenly into prepared pan. Bake 15 minutes or until set.

4. Meanwhile, in medium saucepan, combine cranberries, corn syrup and water. Cook over medium heat, stirring occasionally, until mixture boils. Reduce heat; simmer 15 minutes, stirring occasionally. Remove from heat. Stir in vanilla. Spread evenly over baked layer. Sprinkle reserved 1-1/2 cups crumb topping evenly over top.

5. Return to oven. Bake 15 to 20 minutes or until set. Cool completely in pan on wire rack. Cut into bars.

lemon cheese bars

1 package (about 18 ounces) white or yellow cake mix with pudding in the mix

2 eggs

1/3 cup vegetable oil

1 package (8 ounces) cream cheese, softened

1/3 cup sugar

1 teaspoon lemon juice

Makes about 2 dozen bars

1. Preheat oven to 350°F.

2. Combine cake mix, 1 egg and oil in large bowl; stir until crumbly. Reserve 1 cup crumb mixture. Press remaining crumb mixture into ungreased 13×9-inch baking pan. Bake 15 minutes or until light golden brown.

3. Beat remaining egg, cream cheese, sugar and lemon juice in medium bowl with electric mixer at medium speed until smooth and well blended. Spread over crust. Sprinkle with reserved crumb mixture.

4. Bake 15 minutes or until cream cheese layer is just set. Cool in pan on wire rack. Cut into bars.

thick and fudgey brownies with
HERSHEY'S MINI KISSES® milk chocolates

2-1/4 cups all-purpose flour

2/3 cup HERSHEY'S Cocoa

1 teaspoon baking powder

1 teaspoon salt

3/4 cup (1-1/2 sticks) butter or margarine, melted

2-1/2 cups sugar

2 teaspoons vanilla extract

4 eggs

1-3/4 cups (10-ounce package) HERSHEY'S MINI
    KISSES® Brand Milk Chocolates

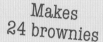

Makes
24 brownies

1. Heat oven to 350°F. (325°F. for glass baking dish). Grease 13×9×2-inch baking pan.

2. Stir together flour, cocoa, baking powder and salt. With spoon or whisk, stir together butter, sugar and vanilla in large bowl. Add eggs; stir until well blended. Stir in flour mixture, blending well. Stir in chocolate pieces. Spread batter in prepared pan.

3. Bake 30 to 35 minutes or until brownies begin to pull away from sides of pan. Cool completely in pan on wire rack; cut into 2-inch squares.

tri-layer chocolate oatmeal bars

CRUST

1 cup uncooked rolled oats

1/2 cup all-purpose flour

1/2 cup firmly packed light brown sugar

1/4 cup MOTT'S® Natural Apple Sauce

1 tablespoon margarine, melted

1/4 teaspoon baking soda

FILLING

2/3 cup all-purpose flour

1/2 teaspoon baking powder

1/4 teaspoon salt

3/4 cup granulated sugar

1/4 cup MOTT'S® Natural Apple Sauce

1 whole egg

1 egg white

2 tablespoons unsweetened cocoa powder

1 tablespoon margarine, melted

1/2 teaspoon vanilla extract

1/4 cup low fat buttermilk

ICING

1 cup powdered sugar

1 tablespoon unsweetened cocoa powder

1 tablespoon skim milk

1 teaspoon instant coffee powder

Makes
14 servings

1. Preheat oven to 350°F. Spray 8-inch square baking pan with nonstick cooking spray.

2. To prepare crust, in medium bowl, combine oats, 1/2 cup flour, brown sugar, 1/4 cup apple sauce, 1 tablespoon margarine and baking soda. Stir with fork until mixture resembles coarse crumbs. Press evenly into bottom of prepared pan. Bake 10 minutes.

3. To prepare filling, in small bowl, combine 2/3 cup flour, baking powder and salt.

4. In large bowl, combine granulated sugar, 1/4 cup apple sauce, whole egg, egg white, 2 tablespoons cocoa, 1 tablespoon margarine and vanilla.

5. Add flour mixture to apple sauce mixture alternately with buttermilk; stir until well blended. Spread filling over baked crust.

6. Bake 25 minutes or until toothpick inserted into center comes out clean. Cool completely on wire rack.

7. To prepare icing, in small bowl, combine powdered sugar, 1 tablespoon cocoa, milk and coffee powder until smooth. Spread evenly over bars. Let stand until set. Run tip of knife through icing to score. Cut into 14 bars.

1 cup all-purpose flour

1/3 cup unsweetened Dutch-process cocoa powder

1/2 teaspoon baking powder

1/2 teaspoon salt

1 cup packed brown sugar

1/2 cup granulated sugar

1/2 cup (1 stick) butter, melted

2 eggs, lightly beaten

1 cup peanut butter chips

1/2 cup chopped peanuts

Makes
16 brownies

1. Preheat oven to 350°F. Grease 8-inch square baking pan.

2. Combine flour, cocoa, baking powder and salt in medium bowl. Whisk brown sugar, granulated sugar and butter in large bowl until well blended. Add eggs; whisk until well blended. Stir in flour mixture, peanut butter chips and peanuts; mix well. Spread evenly in prepared pan.

3. Bake 30 to 35 minutes or until edges begin to pull away from sides of pan. Cool completely in pan on wire rack.

simply special brownies

1/2 cup (1 stick) butter or margarine

1 package (4 ounces) HERSHEY'S SPECIAL DARK®
   or Semi-Sweet Chocolate Premium Baking Bar,
   broken into pieces

2 eggs

1 teaspoon vanilla extract

3/4 teaspoon powdered instant coffee

2/3 cup sugar

1/2 cup all-purpose flour

1/4 teaspoon baking soda

1/4 teaspoon salt

1/2 cup coarsely chopped nuts (optional)

Makes
20 brownies

1. Heat oven to 350°F. Grease 9-inch square baking pan.

2. Place butter and chocolate in medium microwave-safe bowl. Microwave at MEDIUM (50%) 1 minute; stir. If necessary, microwave an additional 15 seconds at a time, stirring after each heating, until chocolate is melted and mixture is smooth when stirred. Add eggs, vanilla and instant coffee, stirring until well blended. Stir in sugar, flour, baking soda and salt; blend completely. Stir in nuts, if desired. Spread batter in prepared pan.

3. Bake 25 to 30 minutes or until wooden pick inserted in center comes out almost clean. Cool completely in pan on wire rack. Cut into bars.

brownies *and* Bars

creamy lemon bars

1 package (2-layer size) lemon cake mix

3 large eggs, divided

1/2 cup oil

2 packages (8 ounces each) PHILADELPHIA® Cream Cheese, softened

1 container (8 ounces) BREAKSTONE'S® or KNUDSEN® Sour Cream

1/2 cup granulated sugar

1 teaspoon grated lemon peel

1 tablespoon lemon juice

Powdered sugar

Makes
2 dozen bars

MIX cake mix, 1 of the eggs and oil. Press mixture onto bottom and up sides of lightly greased 15×10×1-inch baking pan. Bake at 350°F for 10 minutes.

MIX cream cheese with electric mixer on medium speed until smooth. Add remaining 2 eggs, sour cream, granulated sugar, lemon peel and juice; mix until blended. Pour batter into crust.

BAKE at 350°F for 30 to 35 minutes or until filling is just set in center and edges are light golden brown. Cool. Sprinkle with powdered sugar. Cut into bars.

Storage Know-How: Store leftover bars in tightly covered container in refrigerator.

Prep Time: 15 minutes
Bake Time: 35 minutes

caramel chocolate chunk blondies

1-1/2 cups all-purpose flour

1 teaspoon baking powder

1/2 teaspoon salt

3/4 cup granulated sugar

3/4 cup packed brown sugar

1/2 cup (1 stick) butter, softened

2 eggs

1-1/2 teaspoons vanilla

1-1/2 cups semisweet chocolate chunks

1/3 cup caramel ice cream topping

Makes about 2-1/2 dozen blondies

1. Preheat oven to 350°F. Spray 13×9-inch baking pan with nonstick cooking spray.

2. Combine flour, baking powder and salt in medium bowl. Beat granulated sugar, brown sugar and butter in large bowl with electric mixer at medium speed until smooth and creamy. Beat in eggs and vanilla until well blended. Add flour mixture; beat at low speed until blended. Stir in chocolate chunks.

3. Spread batter evenly in prepared pan. Drop spoonfuls of caramel topping over batter; swirl into batter with knife.

4. Bake 25 minutes or until golden brown. Cool completely in pan on wire rack.

double chip brownies

3/4 cup HERSHEY'S Cocoa

1/2 teaspoon baking soda

2/3 cup (1-1/3 sticks) butter or margarine, melted and divided

1/2 cup boiling water

2 cups sugar

2 eggs

1-1/3 cups all-purpose flour

1 teaspoon vanilla extract

1/4 teaspoon salt

1 cup HERSHEY'S Milk Chocolate Chips

1 cup REESE'S® Peanut Butter Chips

Makes about 36 brownies

1. Heat oven to 350°F. Grease 13×9×2-inch baking pan.

2. Stir together cocoa and baking soda in large bowl; stir in 1/3 cup melted butter. Add boiling water; stir until mixture thickens. Stir in sugar, eggs and remaining 1/3 cup melted butter; stir until smooth. Add flour, vanilla and salt; blend thoroughly. Stir in milk chocolate chips and peanut butter chips. Spread in prepared pan.

3. Bake 35 to 40 minutes or until brownies begin to pull away from sides of pan. Cool completely in pan on wire rack. Cut into squares.

chocolate chip candy cookie bars

1-2/3 cups all-purpose flour

2 tablespoons plus 1-1/2 cups sugar, divided

3/4 teaspoon baking powder

1 cup (2 sticks) cold butter or margarine, divided

1 egg, slightly beaten

1/2 cup plus 2 tablespoons (5-ounce can) evaporated milk, divided

2 cups (12-ounce package) HERSHEY'S SPECIAL DARK® Chocolate Chips or HERSHEY'S Semi-Sweet Chocolate Chips, divided

1/2 cup light corn syrup

1-1/2 cups sliced almonds

Makes about 48 bars

1. Heat oven to 375°F.

2. Stir together flour, 2 tablespoons sugar and baking powder in medium bowl; using pastry blender, cut in 1/2 cup butter until mixture forms coarse crumbs. Stir in egg and 2 tablespoons evaporated milk; stir until mixture holds together in ball shape. Press onto bottom and 1/4 inch up sides of 15-1/2 × 10-1/2 × 1-inch jelly-roll pan.

3. Bake 8 to 10 minutes or until lightly browned; remove from oven, leaving oven on. Sprinkle 1-1/2 cups chocolate chips evenly over crust; do not disturb chips.

4. Place remaining 1-1/2 cups sugar, remaining 1/2 cup butter, remaining 1/2 cup evaporated milk and corn syrup in 3-quart saucepan. Cook over medium heat, stirring constantly, until mixture boils; stir in almonds. Continue cooking and stirring to 240°F on candy thermometer (soft-ball stage) or until small amount of mixture, when dropped into very cold water, forms a soft ball which flattens when removed from water. (Bulb of candy thermometer should not rest on bottom of saucepan.) Remove from heat. Immediately spoon almond mixture evenly over chips and crust; do not spread.

5. Bake 10 to 15 minutes or just until almond mixture is golden brown. Remove from oven; cool 5 minutes. Sprinkle remaining 1/2 cup chips over top; cool completely. Cut into bars.

double-chocolate pecan brownies

3/4 cup all-purpose flour

3/4 cup unsweetened cocoa powder

1/2 cup CREAM OF WHEAT® Hot Cereal (Instant, 1-minute, 2-1/2-minute or 10-minute cook time), uncooked

1/2 teaspoon baking powder

1-1/4 cups sugar

1/2 cup (1 stick) butter, softened

2 eggs

1 teaspoon vanilla extract

1/2 cup semisweet chocolate chips

1/2 cup pecans, chopped

1. Preheat oven to 350°F. Line 8-inch square baking pan with foil, extending foil over sides of pan; spray with nonstick cooking spray. Combine flour, cocoa, Cream of Wheat and baking powder in medium bowl; set aside.

2. Cream sugar and butter in large mixing bowl with electric mixer at medium speed. Add eggs and vanilla; mix until well combined.

3. Gradually add Cream of Wheat mixture; mix well. Spread batter evenly in pan, using spatula. Sprinkle chocolate chips and pecans evenly over top.

4. Bake 35 minutes. Let stand 5 minutes. Lift brownies from pan using aluminum foil. Cool completely before cutting.

Prep Time: 15 minutes

Start to Finish Time: 1 hour

Makes
9 brownies

For an even more decadent dessert,
drizzle caramel sauce over the warm brownies
and serve with mint chocolate chip ice cream.

candy
Store

tropical sugarplums

1/2 cup white chocolate chips

1/4 cup light corn syrup

1/2 cup chopped dates

1/4 cup chopped maraschino cherries, well drained

1 teaspoon vanilla

1/4 teaspoon rum extract

1-1/4 cups gingersnap cookie crumbs

Flaked coconut

Makes about 2 dozen

1. Combine white chocolate chips and corn syrup in large saucepan. Cook and stir over low heat until melted and smooth.

2. Stir in dates, cherries, vanilla and rum extract until well blended. Add gingersnap crumbs; stir until well blended. (Mixture will be stiff.)

3. Shape mixture into 3/4-inch balls; roll in coconut. Place in miniature paper candy cups, if desired. Serve immediately or let stand overnight to allow flavors to blend.

Prep Time: 20 minutes

toffee chocolate crispies

1 cup slivered almonds

1 cup crisp rice cereal

1/2 cup milk chocolate toffee bits

1 cup milk or semisweet chocolate chips

1 teaspoon shortening

1. Line baking sheet or large tray with foil. Place almonds in medium nonstick skillet; toast over medium heat, stirring frequently, 7 to 8 minutes or until lightly browned. Pour almonds into large bowl; stir in cereal and toffee bits.

2. Place chocolate chips and shortening in medium microwavable bowl. Microwave on HIGH 20 seconds; stir to blend. Microwave 10 seconds more; stir until smooth. Pour chocolate mixture over almond mixture; stir until evenly coated.

3. Drop mixture by rounded tablespoonfuls onto prepared baking sheet. Refrigerate 30 minutes or until cool and solid. Serve immediately or store between layers of waxed paper in airtight container in refrigerator up to 1 week.

Prep Time: 15 minutes

Chill Time: 30 minutes

Makes about
2 dozen

candy crunch

4 cups (half of 15-ounce bag) pretzel sticks or pretzel twists

4 cups (24 ounces) white chocolate chips

1 (14-ounce) can EAGLE BRAND® Sweetened Condensed Milk (NOT evaporated milk)

1 cup dried fruit (dried cranberries, raisins or mixed dried fruit bits)

1. Place pretzels in large bowl.

2. In large saucepan over low heat, melt white chocolate chips with EAGLE BRAND®. Cook and stir constantly until smooth. Pour over pretzels, stirring to coat.

3. Immediately spread mixture into foil-lined 15×10-inch jelly-roll pan. Sprinkle with dried fruit; press down lightly with back of spoon. Chill 1 to 2 hours or until set. Break into chunks. Store leftovers loosely covered at room temperature.

Prep Time: 10 minutes

Chill Time: 1 to 2 hours

Makes about 1-1/2 pounds

super chunky fudge

1 bag (5.1 ounces) PEPPERIDGE FARM® 100 Calorie Pack Chocolate Chunk Cookies, coarsely crumbled (about 2 cups)

1 cup miniature marshmallows

Vegetable cooking spray

3 cups (18 ounces) semi-sweet chocolate pieces

1 can (14 ounces) sweetened condensed milk

1/8 teaspoon salt

1 teaspoon vanilla extract

1. Reserve **1/2 cup** crumbled cookies and **1/4 cup** marshmallows. Line an 8-inch square baking pan with foil. Spray the foil with cooking spray. Heat the chocolate, milk and salt in a 2-quart saucepan over low heat until the chocolate melts, stirring often.

2. Remove the chocolate mixture from the heat and stir in remaining crumbled cookies, remaining marshmallows and vanilla. Spread the mixture evenly into the prepared pan. Press the reserved cookies and marshmallows into top of fudge.

3. Refrigerate for 2 hours or until firm. Remove fudge from pan and peel away foil. Cut into 16 squares. Wrap in foil. Store in the refrigerator.

Prep Time: 15 minutes

Cook Time: 10 minutes

Chill Time: 2 hours

Makes
2 pounds

Use the gift-wrapping idea pictured above or arrange each piece of fudge in a decorative paper cupcake liner. Wrap with colored plastic wrap and close with a twist-tie or ribbon.

candy Store

creamy almond candy

1-1/2 pounds vanilla-flavored candy coating*

1 (14-ounce) can EAGLE BRAND® Sweetened Condensed Milk (NOT evaporated milk)

1/8 teaspoon salt

3 cups (about 1 pound) whole almonds, toasted**

1 teaspoon almond extract

*Also called confectioners' coating.

**To toast almonds, spread in single layer in heavy-bottomed skillet. Cook over medium heat 2 to 3 minutes, stirring frequently, until nuts are lightly browned. Remove from skillet immediately. Cool before using.

1. In heavy saucepan over low heat, melt candy coating with EAGLE BRAND® and salt. Remove from heat; stir in almonds and almond extract.

2. Spread evenly into wax paper-lined 15×10-inch jelly-roll pan. Chill 2 hours or until firm.

3. Turn onto cutting board; peel off paper and cut into triangles or squares. Store leftovers tightly covered at room temperature.

Microwave Method: In 2-quart glass measure, combine candy coating, EAGLE BRAND® and salt. Microwave on HIGH (100% power) 3 to 5 minutes, stirring after each 1-1/2 minutes. Stir until smooth. Proceed as directed above.

Prep Time: 10 minutes

Chill Time: 2 hours

Makes about 3-1/4 pounds

caramel pecan bonbons

1 package (14 ounces) caramels

1/3 cup whipping cream

3 tablespoons butter

1 tablespoon light corn syrup

1-1/2 cups pecan halves, toasted* and finely chopped

4 ounces dried apple rings, finely chopped

1-1/2 pounds premium milk chocolate, melted

To toast pecans, spread in single layer on ungreased baking sheet. Bake in preheated 350°F oven 8 to 10 minutes or until fragrant, stirring occasionally.

1. Lightly butter 8-inch square pan. Line pan with 12-inch-wide strip of waxed paper, leaving 1-inch overhang on sides to use for handles. Lightly butter waxed paper.

2. Unwrap caramels; place in large heavy saucepan. Add cream, butter and corn syrup; cook over low heat until melted and smooth, stirring often. Remove from heat; stir in pecans and apple rings. Pour caramel mixture into prepared pan; cover and refrigerate 2 hours or until cold and firm.

3. Turn out caramel block onto cutting board by lifting caramel and waxed paper using handles. Peel away waxed paper. Cut caramel block into 1-inch squares. Roll each square into a ball; place on baking sheet lined with waxed paper. Refrigerate 1 hour.

4. Dip balls in melted chocolate with dipping fork or spoon, tapping handle against side of pan to allow excess chocolate to drain back into pan. Remove excess chocolate by scraping bottom of bonbon across rim of saucepan.*

5. Place bonbons on waxed paper; let stand in cool place until chocolate is firm. *Do not refrigerate.* Store in airtight container at room temperature.

Pour any remaining chocolate onto foil; wrap tightly. Chop before remelting.

Makes about 2-1/2 pounds

chocolate-cherry balls

1 cup chocolate graham cracker crumbs
   (6 to 7 crackers)

1 cup mini chocolate chips

3/4 cup butter cookie
   crumbs (8 to 10 cookies)

1/8 teaspoon salt

1/2 cup thick chocolate fudge frosting

1/4 cup dark corn syrup

1 teaspoon vanilla

About 72 dried cherries

1/2 cup powdered sugar

Makes about 3 dozen

1. Combine graham cracker crumbs, chocolate chips, cookie crumbs and salt in large bowl; stir well.

2. Add fudge frosting, corn syrup and vanilla. Knead by hand until the mixture comes together. Shape into 1-inch balls. Press 2 dried cherries into center of each ball and reshape mixture around cherries to cover.

3. Spread powdered sugar on baking sheet; roll balls in sugar to coat.

Variation: Roll balls in unsweetened cocoa powder.

peppermint taffy

2 tablespoons butter, softened and divided

1/2 cup powdered sugar

2-1/2 cups granulated sugar

1/2 cup water

1/4 cup distilled white vinegar

7 to 8 drops red food coloring

1/2 teaspoon peppermint extract

Makes about 1 pound

1. Butter 12-inch ceramic oval platter or dish with 1 tablespoon butter. Line large baking sheet with foil; sprinkle evenly with powdered sugar.

2. Combine granulated sugar, water, vinegar and remaining 1 tablespoon butter in large heavy saucepan. Bring to a boil, stirring frequently. Attach candy thermometer to side of pan, making sure bulb is submerged in sugar mixture but not touching bottom of pan. Continue boiling, without stirring, about 10 minutes or until sugar mixture reaches between hard-ball stage (265°F) and soft-crack stage (270°F) on candy thermometer. Remove from heat; stir in food coloring and peppermint extract.

3. Slowly pour hot sugar mixture onto prepared platter. Let stand 20 to 25 minutes or until cool enough to handle and indent made with your finger holds its shape.

4. Carefully pick up taffy with buttered hands; shape into a ball. (Center of candy may still be very warm but will cool quickly upon handling.) Scrape up any taffy that sticks to plate with rubber spatula.

Be careful not to burn yourself while pulling the taffy! The candy may feel cool on the surface, but it can be burning hot underneath. To prevent burns, make sure your hands are well buttered so the sugar does not stick to your skin. Or, you may wear rubber gloves.

5. Begin to pull taffy between your hands into thick rope about 18 inches long while turning and twisting taffy back on itself. Continue pulling taffy about 10 to 15 minutes or until it lightens in color, has satiny finish and is stiff. (It is important to pull taffy long enough or it will be sticky.)

6. When taffy begins to hold the folds of the rope shape and develops ridges in the rope, begin pulling 1-inch-wide ropes from taffy and let ropes fall onto prepared powdered sugar surface. Cut each rope with buttered kitchen shears. Cut taffy ropes into 1-inch pieces using shears. Cool completely; wrap pieces individually in waxed paper. Store in airtight container at room temperature up to 1 week.

Lemon Taffy: Substitute 4 to 5 drops yellow food coloring for red food coloring and lemon extract for peppermint extract. Proceed as directed.

dark chocolate, almond and apricot bark

3/4 cup whole unblanched almonds, toasted*

3/4 cup dried apricots, chopped

10 ounces semisweet or bittersweet chocolate, chopped (about 2-1/4 cups)

To toast almonds, spread in single layer on ungreased baking sheet. Bake in preheated 350°F oven 8 to 10 minutes or until fragrant, stirring occasionally.

1. Combine almonds and apricots in large bowl. Line large baking sheet with waxed paper.

2. Melt about three fourths of chocolate in top of double boiler over hot, not boiling, water, stirring frequently. Remove from heat. Add one third of remaining chocolate to melted chocolate; stir until melted. Repeat twice.

3. Add almond and apricot mixture to chocolate; stir until completely coated. Spread mixture evenly on prepared baking sheet. Refrigerate 30 minutes. Peel off waxed paper; break or cut into 1- to 1-1/2-inch pieces. Store between sheets of waxed paper in airtight container at room temperature for up to 2 weeks.

Makes about
3 dozen

chocolate & peanut butter truffles

3/4 cup (1-1/2 sticks) butter (no substitutes)

1 cup REESE'S® Peanut Butter Chips

1/2 cup HERSHEY'S Cocoa

1 can (14 ounces) sweetened condensed milk (not evaporated milk)

1 tablespoon vanilla extract

HERSHEY'S Cocoa or finely chopped nuts or graham cracker crumbs

1. Melt butter and peanut butter chips in saucepan over very low heat. Add cocoa; stir until smooth. Add sweetened condensed milk; stir constantly until mixture is thick and glossy, about 4 minutes. Remove from heat; stir in vanilla.

2. Refrigerate 2 hours or until firm enough to handle. Shape into 1-inch balls; roll in cocoa, nuts or graham cracker crumbs. Refrigerate until firm, about 1 hour. Store, covered, in refrigerator.

Prep Time: 30 minutes

Cook Time: 7 minutes

Chill Time: 3 hours

Makes about 3-1/2 dozen

malted milk balls

2-1/2 cups small malted milk balls (1/2-inch diameter), coarsely crushed

1-3/4 cups chocolate graham cracker crumbs (9 to 11 crackers)

3 tablespoons unsweetened cocoa powder

1/4 teaspoon salt

1 cup mini marshmallows

1/2 cup light corn syrup

1 tablespoon honey

1 teaspoon rum extract

1/2 cup powdered sugar

Makes about 4 dozen

1. Combine malted milk balls, graham cracker crumbs, cocoa and salt in large bowl; stir well. Chop marshmallows; add to bowl.

2. Add corn syrup, honey and rum extract. Knead by hand until mixture comes together. Shape into 1-inch balls.

3. Spread powdered sugar on baking sheet; roll balls in sugar to coat.

Variation: Roll balls in unsweetened cocoa powder. Substitute 1 teaspoon vanilla for the rum extract.

To easily make graham cracker crumbs, place them in a resealable food storage bag, and use a rolling pin to crush the crackers into fine crumbs. The malted milk balls can also be crushed in a resealable food storage bag.

candy Store

festive fudge

3 cups (18 ounces) semisweet or milk chocolate chips

1 (14-ounce) can EAGLE BRAND® Sweetened Condensed Milk (NOT evaporated milk)

Dash salt

1/2 to 1 cup chopped nuts (optional)

1-1/2 teaspoons vanilla extract

Makes about 2 pounds

1. Line 8- or 9-inch square pan with wax paper. In heavy saucepan over low heat, melt chocolate chips with EAGLE BRAND® and salt. Remove from heat; stir in nuts (optional) and vanilla. Spread evenly in prepared pan. Chill 2 hours or until firm.

2. Turn fudge onto cutting board; peel off paper and cut into squares. Store leftovers covered in refrigerator.

Chocolate Peanut Butter Chip Glazed Fudge: Proceed as above, but substitute 3/4 cup peanut butter chips for nuts. For glaze, melt additional 1/2 cup peanut butter chips with 1/2 cup whipping cream; stir until thick and smooth. Spread over chilled fudge.

Marshmallow Fudge: Proceed as above, but add 2 tablespoons butter to chocolate mixture, and fold in 2 cups miniature marshmallows instead of nuts.

Gift Tips: Create delicious homemade gifts from an assortment of flavored fudges, packed in decorative tins, candy bags or boxes. Wrap individual pieces of fudge in colored food-grade cellophane, candy wrappers or gold or silver foil candy cups and arrange in gift bags or tins. Store in refrigerator.

Prep Time: 10 minutes

breads
and Muffins

pineapple orange walnut bread

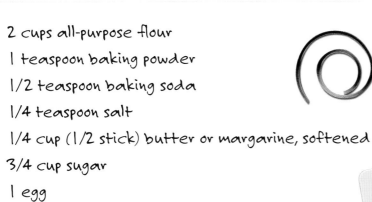

2 cups all-purpose flour

1 teaspoon baking powder

1/2 teaspoon baking soda

1/4 teaspoon salt

1/4 cup (1/2 stick) butter or margarine, softened

3/4 cup sugar

1 egg

1 tablespoon grated orange peel

1/4 cup orange juice

1 can (8 ounces) DOLE® Crushed Pineapple, undrained

1 cup DOLE® Seedless or Golden Raisins

1 cup chopped walnuts, toasted

Makes 12 servings

• Combine flour, baking powder, baking soda and salt in medium bowl; set aside.

• Beat together butter and sugar in large bowl until light and fluffy. Beat in egg, orange peel and orange juice. Alternately stir in one-third flour mixture and one-half undrained crushed pineapple until just blended, ending with flour. Stir in raisins and walnuts.

• Pour batter into 9×5-inch loaf pan sprayed with nonstick vegetable cooking spray.

• Bake at 350°F 60 minutes or until toothpick inserted in center comes out clean. Cool in pan 10 minutes. Remove from pan to wire rack; cool completely.

Prep Time: 20 minutes

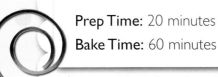

Bake Time: 60 minutes

chocolate oatmeal walnut muffins

1 cup quick-cooking rolled oats

1 cup buttermilk or sour milk*

2/3 cup light brown sugar, packed

1/3 cup vegetable oil

1 egg

1 teaspoon vanilla extract

3/4 cup all-purpose flour

1/4 cup HERSHEY'S Cocoa

1 teaspoon baking powder

1 teaspoon salt

1/2 teaspoon baking soda

1 cup coarsely chopped walnuts

Powdered sugar (optional)

*To sour milk: Use 1 tablespoon white vinegar plus milk to equal 1 cup.

Makes about 14 muffins

1. Heat oven to 400°F. Grease or line muffin cups (2-1/2-inches in diameter) with paper bake cups.

2. Stir together oats and buttermilk in small bowl; let stand 20 minutes.

3. Stir together brown sugar, oil, egg and vanilla in large bowl. Add oats mixture, stirring well. Stir together flour, cocoa, baking powder, salt and baking soda. Add to oats mixture, blending until moistened. Stir in nuts. Fill muffin cups 2/3 full with batter.

4. Bake 16 to 18 minutes or until wooden pick inserted in centers comes out clean. Remove from pan to wire rack. Sprinkle muffin tops with powdered sugar, if desired. Serve warm or cool.

loaded banana bread

6 tablespoons butter, softened

1/3 cup packed light brown sugar

1/3 cup granulated sugar

2 eggs

3 ripe bananas, mashed

1/2 teaspoon vanilla

1-1/2 cups all-purpose flour

2-1/2 teaspoons baking powder

1/4 teaspoon salt

1 can (8 ounces) crushed pineapple, drained

1/3 cup flaked sweetened coconut

1/4 cup mini chocolate chips

1/3 cup chopped walnuts (optional)

Makes 1 loaf

1. Preheat oven to 350°F. Grease or coat 9×5-inch nonstick loaf pan with nonstick cooking spray; set aside.

2. Beat butter, brown sugar and granulated sugar in large bowl with electric mixer on medium speed until light and fluffy. Mix in eggs, one at a time, scraping bowl after each addition. Add bananas and vanilla. Beat until just combined.

3. Sift together flour, baking powder and salt in small bowl. Gradually beat flour mixture into banana mixture until just combined. Fold in pineapple, coconut and chocolate chips.

4. Spoon batter into prepared loaf pan. Top with walnuts, if desired. Bake 50 minutes or until toothpick inserted into center comes out almost clean. Let cool 1 hour; remove from pan.

jumbo streusel-topped raspberry muffins

2-1/4 cups all-purpose flour, divided

1/4 cup packed brown sugar

2 tablespoons cold butter

3/4 cup granulated sugar

2 teaspoons baking powder

1/2 teaspoon baking soda

1/2 teaspoon salt

1/2 teaspoon grated lemon peel

3/4 cup plus 2 tablespoons milk

1/3 cup butter, melted

1 egg, beaten

2 cups fresh or frozen raspberries (do not thaw)

Makes 6 jumbo muffins

1. Preheat oven to 350°F. Grease 6 jumbo (3-1/2-inch) muffin cups.

2. For topping, combine 1/4 cup flour and brown sugar in small bowl. Cut in cold butter with pastry blender or two knives until mixture forms coarse crumbs.

3. Reserve 1/4 cup flour in medium bowl. Combine remaining 1-3/4 cups flour, granulated sugar, baking powder, baking soda, salt and lemon peel in medium bowl. Combine milk, melted butter and egg in small bowl.

Choose fresh raspberries that have a rich color and a sweet, berrylike aroma. Avoid berries that have a hull attached in the center. This is a sign that they were picked before fully ripe and are likely to be tart.

4. Add milk mixture to flour mixture; stir until almost blended. Toss raspberries with reserved flour just until coated; gently fold raspberries into muffin batter. Spoon batter into prepared muffin cups, filling three-fourths full. Sprinkle with topping.

5. Bake 25 to 30 minutes or until toothpick inserted into centers comes out clean. Cool in pan 2 minutes; remove to wire rack. Serve warm or at room temperature.

Variation: For smaller muffins, spoon batter into 12 standard (2-1/2-inch) greased or paper-lined muffin cups. Bake at 350°F 21 to 24 minutes or until toothpick inserted into centers comes out clean.

poppy seed bread

Bread

3 cups all-purpose flour

1-1/2 teaspoons salt

1-1/2 teaspoons WATKINS® Baking Powder

2-1/4 cups granulated sugar

3 eggs

1-1/2 cups milk

1 cup plus 2 tablespoons WATKINS® Original Grapeseed Oil

1-1/2 to 4 tablespoons poppy seed

1-1/2 teaspoons WATKINS® Vanilla

1-1/2 teaspoons WATKINS® Almond Extract

1-1/2 teaspoons WATKINS® Butter Extract

Glaze

3/4 cup powdered sugar

1/4 cup orange juice

1/2 teaspoon WATKINS® Vanilla

1/2 teaspoon WATKINS® Almond Extract

1/2 teaspoon WATKINS® Butter Extract

Makes
2 loaves

Preheat oven to 350°F. Grease and flour two 8-1/2×4-1/2-inch loaf pans. Combine all bread ingredients in large bowl in order listed above; beat 2 minutes. Pour into prepared pans. Bake for 55 minutes or until toothpick inserted into centers comes out clean.

Meanwhile, blend all glaze ingredients in small bowl until smooth. Drizzle over bread while loaves are warm.

strawbabies

2 cups all-purpose flour

3/4 cup sugar

2 teaspoons baking powder

3/4 teaspoon baking soda

3/4 teaspoon salt

1 cup coarsely chopped fresh strawberries (about 1 quart)

1 container (8 ounces) strawberry yogurt (blended, not fruit at the bottom)

3/4 cup milk

1/2 cup vegetable oil

1 egg

1/4 teaspoon almond extract

Makes 36 mini muffins

1. Preheat oven to 400°F. Grease 36 mini (1-3/4-inch) muffin cups or line with paper baking cups.

2. Combine flour, sugar, baking powder, baking soda and salt in large bowl. Add strawberries; toss until evenly coated.

3. Beat yogurt, milk, oil, egg and almond extract in medium bowl until well blended. Add to flour mixture; stir gently just until blended. Spoon batter evenly into prepared muffin cups, filling almost full.

4. Bake 10 to 12 minutes or until toothpick inserted into centers comes out clean. Cool muffins in pans 2 minutes; remove to wire racks. Serve warm or at room temperature.

lots o' chocolate bread

2 cups mini semisweet chocolate chips, divided

2/3 cup packed light brown sugar

1/2 cup (1 stick) butter, softened

2 eggs

2-1/2 cups all-purpose flour

1-1/2 cups applesauce

1-1/2 teaspoons vanilla

1 teaspoon baking soda

1 teaspoon baking powder

1/2 teaspoon salt

1 tablespoon shortening (do not use butter, margarine, spread or oil)

Makes 5 mini loaves

1. Preheat oven to 350°F. Grease 5 mini (5-1/2×3-inch) loaf pans. Place 1 cup chocolate chips in small microwavable bowl. Microwave on HIGH 1 minute; stir. Microwave at 30-second intervals, stirring after each interval, until chocolate is melted.

2. Beat brown sugar and butter in large bowl with electric mixer at medium speed until creamy. Add melted chocolate and eggs; beat until well blended. Add flour, applesauce, vanilla, baking soda, baking powder and salt; beat until well blended. Stir in 1/2 cup chocolate chips. Spoon batter evenly into prepared pans.

3. Bake 35 to 40 minutes or until centers crack and are dry to the touch. Cool in pans on wire racks 10 minutes. Remove from pans; cool completely.

4. Place remaining 1/2 cup chocolate chips and shortening in small microwavable bowl. Microwave on HIGH 1 minute; stir. Microwave at 30-second intervals, stirring after each interval, until chocolate is melted and mixture is smooth. Drizzle loaves with glaze; let stand until set.

Wrap each loaf in plastic wrap or cellophane
and place in a colorful gift bag. With each loaf include
a sampling of single-serving packets
of gourmet coffee or tea.

hearty banana carrot muffins

2 ripe, medium DOLE® Bananas

1 package (14 ounces) oat bran muffin mix

3/4 teaspoon ground ginger

1 medium DOLE® Carrot, shredded (1/2 cup)

1/3 cup light molasses

1/3 cup DOLE® Seedless or Golden Raisins

1/4 cup chopped almonds

• Mash bananas with fork (1 cup).

• Combine muffin mix and ginger in large bowl. Add carrot, molasses, raisins and bananas. Stir just until moistened.

• Spoon batter into paper-lined muffin cups. Sprinkle tops with almonds.

• Bake at 425°F 12 to 14 minutes until browned.

Prep Time: 20 minutes

Bake Time: 14 minutes

Makes
12 muffins

chocolate chip elvis bread

2-1/2 cups all-purpose flour

1/2 cup granulated sugar

1/2 cup packed brown sugar

1 tablespoon baking powder

3/4 teaspoon salt

1 cup mashed ripe bananas (about 2 large)

1 cup milk

3/4 cup peanut butter

1/4 cup vegetable oil

1 egg, lightly beaten

1 teaspoon vanilla

1 cup semisweet chocolate chips

Makes
4 mini loaves

1. Preheat oven to 350°F. Spray 4 mini (5-1/2×3-inch) or 3 (7-1/2×3-1/2-inch) loaf pans with nonstick cooking spray.

2. Combine flour, granulated sugar, brown sugar, baking powder and salt in large bowl; mix well. Beat bananas, milk, peanut butter, oil, egg and vanilla in medium bowl until well blended. Add banana mixture and chocolate chips to flour mixture; stir just until moistened. Pour into prepared pans.

3. Bake 40 minutes or until toothpick inserted into centers comes out clean (45 to 50 minutes for 7-1/2×3-1/2-inch pans). Cool in pans on wire racks 10 minutes. Remove from pans; cool completely.

lemon poppy seed muffins

2 cups all-purpose flour

1-1/4 cups granulated sugar

1/4 cup poppy seeds

2 tablespoons plus 2 teaspoons grated lemon peel, divided

2 teaspoons baking powder

1/2 teaspoon baking soda

1/2 teaspoon ground cardamom

1/4 teaspoon salt

2 eggs

1/2 cup (1 stick) butter, melted

1/2 cup milk

1/2 cup plus 2 tablespoons lemon juice, divided

1 cup powdered sugar

Makes 18 muffins

1. Preheat oven to 400°F. Grease 18 standard (2-1/2-inch) muffin cups or line with paper baking cups.

2. Combine flour, granulated sugar, poppy seeds, 2 tablespoons lemon peel, baking powder, baking soda, cardamom and salt in large bowl. Beat eggs in medium bowl. Add butter, milk and 1/2 cup lemon juice; mix well. Add egg mixture to flour mixture; stir just until blended. Spoon batter evenly into prepared muffin cups, filling three-fourths full.

3. Bake 15 to 20 minutes or until toothpick inserted into centers comes out clean. Cool in pans on wire racks 10 minutes.

4. Meanwhile, prepare glaze. Combine powdered sugar and remaining 2 teaspoons lemon peel in small bowl; stir in enough remaining lemon juice to make pourable glaze. Place muffins on sheet of foil or waxed paper; drizzle with glaze. Serve warm or at room temperature.

black forest banana bread

1 jar (10 ounces) maraschino cherries

1-3/4 cups all-purpose flour

2 teaspoons baking powder

1/2 teaspoon salt

2/3 cup packed brown sugar

1/3 cup butter, softened

1 cup mashed ripe bananas (about 2 large)

2 eggs

1 cup semisweet chocolate chips

3/4 cup chopped pecans

Makes 1 loaf

1. Preheat oven to 350°F. Lightly spray 9×5-inch loaf pan with nonstick cooking spray. Drain cherries, reserving 2 tablespoons juice. Coarsely chop cherries.

2. Combine flour, baking powder and salt in medium bowl. Beat brown sugar and butter in large bowl with electric mixer until creamy. Beat in bananas, eggs and reserved cherry juice until well blended. Stir in flour mixture, chopped cherries, chocolate chips and pecans just until blended. Pour into prepared pan.

3. Bake 1 hour or until golden brown and toothpick inserted into center comes out clean. Cool in pan on wire rack 10 minutes. Remove from pan; cool completely.

mixed-up muffins

2 cups all-purpose flour

1 cup sugar, divided

2 teaspoons baking powder

1/2 teaspoon baking soda

1/4 teaspoon salt

1/3 cup mini chocolate chips

1/3 cup unsweetened cocoa powder

1-1/4 cups milk

2 eggs

1/3 cup vegetable oil

1 teaspoon vanilla

Makes
15 muffins

1. Preheat oven to 400°F. Line 15 standard (2-1/2-inch) muffin cups with paper baking cups or spray with nonstick cooking spray.

2. Combine flour, 3/4 cup sugar, baking powder, baking soda and salt in medium bowl. Remove 1-1/2 cups mixture to separate bowl; stir in chocolate chips. Stir cocoa and remaining 1/4 cup sugar into remaining flour mixture.

3. Beat milk, eggs, oil and vanilla in small bowl. Add half of milk mixture to each bowl of dry ingredients. Stir each batter separately just until blended. Spoon white and chocolate batters side by side into prepared muffin cups, filling about three-fourths full.

4. Bake 20 to 25 minutes or until toothpick inserted into centers comes out clean. Cool in pans on wire racks 2 minutes. Serve warm or at room temperature.

orange cranberry-nut bread

2 cups all-purpose flour

1 teaspoon baking powder

1/2 teaspoon baking soda

1/4 teaspoon salt

1/2 cup chopped pecans

1 cup dried cranberries

2 teaspoons dried orange peel

2/3 cup boiling water

3/4 cup sugar

2 tablespoons shortening

1 egg, lightly beaten

1 teaspoon vanilla

Makes 8 to
10 servings

Slow Cooker Directions

1. Coat slow cooker with nonstick cooking spray. Blend flour, baking powder, baking soda and salt in medium bowl. Mix in pecans; set aside.

2. Combine cranberries and orange peel in separate medium bowl; pour boiling water over fruit mixture and stir. Add sugar, shortening, egg and vanilla; stir just until blended. Add flour mixture; stir just until blended.

3. Pour batter into slow cooker. Cover; cook on HIGH 1-1/4 to 1-1/2 hours or until edges begin to brown and toothpick inserted into center comes out clean. Remove stoneware from slow cooker. Cool on wire rack about 10 minutes. Remove from stoneware; cool completely.

Prep Time: 15 minutes

Cook Time: 1-1/4 to 1-1/2 hours (HIGH)

apricot mini muffins

1-1/2 cups all-purpose flour

1/2 cup sugar

1/2 cup finely chopped dried apricots

1/4 teaspoon baking powder

1/4 teaspoon baking soda

1/8 teaspoon salt

Pinch ground nutmeg

1/2 cup (1 stick) butter, melted and cooled

2 eggs

2 tablespoons milk

1 teaspoon vanilla

Makes 2 dozen mini muffins

1. Preheat oven to 350°F. Spray 24 mini (1-3/4-inch) muffin cups with nonstick cooking spray.

2. Combine flour, sugar, apricots, baking powder, baking soda, salt and nutmeg in large bowl; mix well. Whisk butter, eggs, milk and vanilla in medium bowl. Add butter mixture to flour mixture; mix just until blended. Spoon about 1 tablespoon batter into each prepared muffin cup.

3. Bake 12 to 15 minutes or until toothpick inserted into centers comes out clean. Cool in pans 5 minutes. Remove to wire racks; cool completely.

boston black coffee bread

1/2 cup rye flour

1/2 cup cornmeal

1/2 cup whole wheat flour

1 teaspoon baking soda

1/2 teaspoon salt

3/4 cup strong brewed coffee, room temperature
  or cold

1/3 cup molasses

1/4 cup canola oil

3/4 cup raisins

Cream cheese (optional)

Makes 1 loaf

1. Preheat oven to 325°F. Butter and flour 9×4-inch loaf pan; set aside.

2. Combine rye flour, cornmeal, whole wheat flour, baking soda and salt in mixing bowl. Stir in coffee, molasses and oil until mixture forms thick batter. Fold in raisins.

3. Pour batter into prepared loaf pan. Bake 50 minutes or until toothpick inserted into center comes out clean. Cool completely in pan on wire rack. Serve with cream cheese, if desired.

Tip: If coffee is hot, pour over 2 ice cubes in a measuring cup to measure 3/4 cup total. Let stand 10 minutes to cool.

breads *and Muffins*

blueberry white chip muffins

2 cups all-purpose flour

1/2 cup granulated sugar

1/4 cup packed brown sugar

2-1/2 teaspoons baking powder

1/2 teaspoon salt

3/4 cup milk

1 large egg, lightly beaten

1/4 cup (1/2 stick) butter or margarine, melted

1/2 teaspoon grated lemon peel

2 cups (12-ounce package) NESTLÉ® TOLL HOUSE® Premier White Morsels, divided

1-1/2 cups fresh or frozen blueberries

Streusel Topping (recipe follows)

Makes
18 muffins

PREHEAT oven to 375°F. Paper-line 18 muffin cups.

COMBINE flour, granulated sugar, brown sugar, baking powder and salt in large bowl. Stir in milk, egg, butter and lemon peel. Stir in *1-1/2 cups* morsels and blueberries. Spoon into prepared muffin cups, filling almost full. Sprinkle with Streusel Topping.

BAKE for 22 to 25 minutes or until wooden pick inserted into centers comes out clean. Cool in pans for 5 minutes; remove to wire racks to cool slightly.

PLACE *remaining* morsels in small, *heavy-duty* resealable plastic food storage bag. Microwave on MEDIUM–HIGH (70%) power for 30 seconds; knead. Microwave at additional 10- to 15-second intervals, kneading until smooth. Cut tiny corner from bag; squeeze to drizzle over muffins. Serve warm.

Streusel Topping: COMBINE 1/3 cup granulated sugar, 1/4 cup all-purpose flour and 1/4 teaspoon ground cinnamon in small bowl. Cut in 3 tablespoons butter or margarine with pastry blender or two knives until mixture resembles coarse crumbs.

cherry scones

1-1/2 cups all-purpose flour

1 cup whole wheat flour

3 tablespoons sugar

2 teaspoons baking powder

1/4 teaspoon salt

1/2 cup butter-flavored shortening

1/2 cup honey beer

1/3 cup milk

1 egg, beaten

3/4 cup dried cherries

1 teaspoon raw sugar

Fresh fruit and cherry preserves (optional)

Makes 8 scones

1. Preheat oven to 425°F. Combine all-purpose flour, whole wheat flour, sugar, baking powder and salt in large bowl. Cut in shortening until mixture resembles coarse crumbs. Combine beer, milk and egg in medium bowl; stir into flour mixture. Stir in cherries. Turn onto floured surface; knead gently 4 times.

2. Shape dough into ball and place on ungreased baking sheet. Pat into 8-inch circle. Score dough into 8 wedges (do not separate). Sprinkle with raw sugar. Bake 18 to 22 minutes or until golden brown. Cut into wedges. Serve with fruit and preserves, if desired.

orange-chocolate chip muffins

3 cups all-purpose flour

1-1/4 cups sugar

1-1/2 teaspoons baking soda

1 teaspoon baking powder

1/2 teaspoon salt

1-1/4 cups milk

3/4 cup vegetable oil

2 eggs

Grated peel of 1 orange (3 to 4 teaspoons)

1 cup semisweet chocolate chips

Makes 12 muffins

1. Preheat oven to 350°F. Spray 12 standard (2-1/2-inch) muffin cups with nonstick cooking spray or line with paper baking cups.

2. Combine flour, sugar, baking soda, baking powder and salt in large bowl. Mix milk, oil, eggs and orange peel in medium bowl until well blended. Add milk mixture and chocolate chips to flour mixture; stir just until moistened. Spoon evenly into prepared muffin cups, filling about three-fourths full.

3. Bake 25 to 28 minutes or until toothpick inserted into centers comes out clean. Cool in pan on wire rack 5 minutes. Remove from pan; cool completely.

double chocolate zucchini muffins

2-1/3 cups all-purpose flour

1-1/4 cups sugar

1/3 cup unsweetened cocoa powder

2 teaspoons baking powder

1-1/2 teaspoons ground cinnamon

1 teaspoon baking soda

1/2 teaspoon salt

1 cup sour cream

1/2 cup vegetable oil

2 eggs, beaten

1/4 cup milk

1 cup milk chocolate chips

1 cup shredded zucchini

Makes 12 jumbo muffins

1. Preheat oven to 400°F. Line 12 jumbo (3-1/2-inch) muffin cups with paper baking cups or spray with nonstick cooking spray.

2. Combine flour, sugar, cocoa, baking powder, cinnamon, baking soda and salt in large bowl. Combine sour cream, oil, eggs and milk in medium bowl until blended; stir into flour mixture just until moistened. Fold in chocolate chips and zucchini. Spoon batter into prepared muffin cups, filling half full.

3. Bake 25 to 30 minutes or until toothpick inserted into centers comes out clean. Cool in pan on wire rack 5 minutes. Remove from pan; cool completely.

Variation: For standard-size muffins, spoon batter into 18 standard (2-1/2-inch) paper-lined or greased muffin cups. Bake at 400°F 18 to 20 minutes or until toothpick inserted into centers comes out clean.

Store muffins in an airtight plastic bag and they will stay fresh for several days. For longer storage, wrap and freeze. Frozen muffins should be used within one month.

gifts from
a Jar

chocolate rice pudding mix

1/2 cup cornstarch

1/2 cup sugar

1/2 teaspoon salt

1/2 cup semisweet chocolate chips

3/4 cup instant rice

1 bar (3 ounces) premium semisweet chocolate

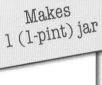

Makes
1 (1-pint) jar

1. Combine cornstarch, sugar and salt in small bowl. Pour into 1-pint wide-mouth jar with tight-fitting lid and pack down firmly. Layer chocolate chips and rice attractively. Pack down lightly before adding each layer. Seal jar.

2. Cover top of jar with fabric. Attach gift tag/recipe with raffia or ribbon. Wrap chocolate bar in matching gift wrap and attach to jar.

chocolate rice pudding

1 quart whole milk

1 jar Chocolate Rice Pudding Mix

1/2 cup whipping cream

1 tablespoon sugar

Makes
6 servings

1. Set aside chocolate bar. Bring milk to a simmer over medium heat in large saucepan. Gradually stir in contents of jar. Cook over medium-low heat, stirring constantly until thickened, about 20 minutes.

2. Spoon pudding into 6 heat-proof cups. Set aside to cool.

3. Beat cream in small bowl with electric mixer at medium speed until soft peaks form. Gradually add sugar and continue beating until stiff. Spoon generous dollop of cream on top of each pudding. Make chocolate shavings from chocolate bar, using vegetable peeler. Sprinkle over whipped cream.

apricot almond bars mix

**Makes
1 (1-quart) jar**

1-3/4 cups all-purpose flour

2 teaspoons baking powder

1 cup chopped dried apricots or dried
    cherries

1/2 cup packed brown sugar

1 cup powdered sugar, divided

1/3 cup sliced almonds

1. Layer flour, baking powder, apricots, brown
sugar and 1/2 cup powdered sugar in 1-quart
food storage jar with tight-fitting lid. Lightly
pack down ingredients before adding another
layer. Place remaining 1/2 cup powdered sugar
and almonds in separate small food storage
bags. Close each bag with twist tie; cut off tops
of bags. Place in jar.

2. Cover top of jar with fabric. Attach gift tag/
recipe with raffia or ribbon.

apricot almond bars

1 jar Apricot Almond Bars Mix

1/2 cup (1 stick) butter, softened

1 egg

1 teaspoon almond extract

1-1/2 teaspoons milk

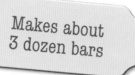

Makes about
3 dozen bars

1. Preheat oven to 350°F. Grease 13×9-inch baking pan.

2. Remove powdered sugar and almond packets from jar. Place remaining contents of jar in medium bowl; stir until well blended. Beat butter, egg and almond extract in large bowl with electric mixer at medium speed. (Mixture may appear curdled.) Add flour mixture; beat just until blended. (Dough will be crumbly.) Press dough into prepared pan; sprinkle with almonds. Bake 25 minutes or until lightly browned. Cool in pan on wire rack.

3. Place powdered sugar in small bowl. Add enough milk to make glaze, stirring until smooth. Drizzle over warm cookies. Cool completely; cut into bars.

Serving Suggestion: To cut these delicious bars into diamond shapes, cut straight lines 1 inch apart along the length of the pan. Then cut straight lines 1-1/2 inches apart diagonally across the pan.

chocolate cherry pancakes mix

2 cups all-purpose flour

1/3 cup sugar

4-1/2 teaspoons baking powder

1/2 teaspoon baking soda

1/2 teaspoon salt

1 cup dried cherries

2/3 cup semisweet chocolate chips

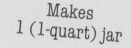

Makes
1 (1-quart) jar

1. Combine flour, sugar, baking powder, baking soda and salt in large bowl. Layer flour mixture, cherries and chocolate chips in 1-quart food storage jar with tight-fitting lid. Pack ingredients down lightly before adding another layer. Seal jar.

2. Cover top of jar with fabric. Attach gift tag/recipe with raffia or ribbon.

chocolate cherry pancakes

2 eggs, beaten

1/4 cup (1/2 stick) butter, melted

1 jar Chocolate Cherry Pancakes Mix

1-1/2 to 2 cups milk

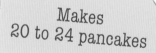

Makes
20 to 24 pancakes

1. Combine eggs and melted butter in large bowl. Add contents of jar; stir until well blended. Add 1-1/2 cups milk; stir until dry ingredients are moistened. Add additional milk if thinner pancakes are desired.

2. Heat griddle or large nonstick skillet until a drop of water sizzles. Pour batter onto hot griddle 1/4 cup at a time. Cook pancakes until golden on both sides.

peanutty double chip cookies mix

2 cups all-purpose flour

1 cup milk chocolate chips

3/4 cup granulated sugar

3/4 cup packed light brown sugar

1/2 cup peanut butter chips

1 teaspoon baking soda

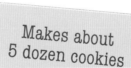
Makes
1 (1-quart) jar

1. Layer ingredients attractively in any order in 1-quart food storage jar with tight-fitting lid. Pack ingredients down lightly before adding another layer. Seal jar.

2. Cover top of jar with fabric. Attach gift tag/recipe with raffia or ribbon.

peanutty double chip cookies

1/2 cup (1 stick) butter, softened

2 eggs

1 teaspoon vanilla

1 cup chunky peanut butter

1 jar Peanutty Double Chip Cookies Mix

Makes about
5 dozen cookies

1. Preheat oven to 350°F. Lightly grease cookie sheets or line with parchment paper.

2. Beat butter in large bowl with electric mixer at medium speed until smooth. Beat in eggs, one at a time, until well blended. Beat in vanilla. (Mixture may appear curdled.) Beat in peanut butter until well blended. Place contents of jar in separate large bowl; mix well. Stir dry ingredients into butter mixture until well blended. Shape dough into 2-inch balls; place 2 inches apart on prepared cookie sheets. Flatten slightly with fork.

3. Bake 12 minutes or until just golden at edges. *Do not overbake.* Remove to wire racks to cool completely.

savory wild rice salad mix

1 tablespoon dehydrated chopped parsley

1/4 teaspoon salt

1/4 teaspoon black pepper

1/4 teaspoon dried thyme

1 package (6.2 ounces) long-grain and wild rice mix (fast-cook recipe)

1/4 cup chopped sun-dried tomatoes (not packed in oil)

1/4 cup dehydrated chopped chives

1/2 cup coarsely chopped pecans or hazelnuts

Makes
1 (1-pint) jar

1. Combine parsley, salt, pepper and thyme in small bowl. Pour mixture into 1-pint wide-mouth jar with tight-fitting lid.

2. Discard rice seasoning packet or save for another recipe. Layer rice, sun-dried tomatoes, chives and pecans attractively in jar. Pack down lightly before adding each layer. Seal jar.

3. Cover top of jar with fabric. Attach gift tag/recipe with raffia or ribbon. Attach large wooden salad spoon, if desired.

There are two secrets to cooking perfect rice. Use very low heat and do not open the saucepan until the cooking time is complete. Opening the saucepan before the rice is done lets the heat escape and causes unappealing texture.

savory wild rice salad

1 jar Savory Wild Rice Salad Mix

1 medium red bell pepper, finely diced

1/4 cup finely chopped green onions

1 tablespoon white wine vinegar

1/2 to 3/4 teaspoon salt

1/4 teaspoon black pepper

3 tablespoons olive oil

Makes 6 to 8 servings

1. Combine 1-3/4 cups water and Savory Wild Rice Salad Mix in large saucepan. Bring to a boil. Cover and reduce heat to low. Simmer 10 to 12 minutes or until rice is tender. Remove from heat. Let stand 5 minutes.

2. Transfer to salad bowl; cool to room temperature. Stir in bell pepper and green onions.

3. Combine vinegar, salt and black pepper in small bowl, stirring until salt dissolves. Blend in oil. Add to salad and mix.

1-1/4 cups flour

1/2 teaspoon baking powder

1/4 teaspoon baking soda

1/4 teaspoon salt

1/3 cup packed brown sugar

1/3 cup granulated sugar

1/2 cup chocolate-covered toffee chips

3/4 cup mini candy-coated chocolate pieces

1/2 cup peanut butter and milk chocolate chips

1/2 cup lightly salted peanuts, coarsely chopped

1. Combine flour, baking powder, baking soda and salt in large bowl. Spoon flour mixture into 1-quart food storage jar with tight-fitting lid. Layer remaining ingredients on top of flour. Pack ingredients down lightly before adding another layer. Seal jar.

2. Cover top of jar with fabric. Attach gift tag/recipe to jar with raffia or ribbon.

Makes
1 (1-quart) jar

happy birthday cookies

1/2 cup (1 stick) butter, softened

1 egg

1/2 teaspoon vanilla

1 jar Happy Birthday Cookies Mix

Makes 3 dozen cookies

1. Preheat oven to 375°F. Line cookie sheets with parchment paper.

2. Beat butter in large bowl with electric mixer at medium speed until fluffy. Beat in egg and vanilla. Add contents of jar to butter mixture; beat 1 minute or until dough forms.

3. Drop dough by rounded tablespoonfuls 2 inches apart onto prepared cookie sheets. Bake 10 minutes or until firm and golden brown. Cool on cookie sheets 1 minute. Remove to wire racks to cool completely.

apricot-cranberry bread mix

2-1/2 cups all-purpose flour

1 cup chopped dried apricots

3/4 cup sugar

1/2 cup dried cranberries

4 teaspoons baking powder

1/2 teaspoon baking soda

1/2 teaspoon salt

Makes
1 (1-quart) jar

1. Layer ingredients attractively in any order in 1-quart food storage jar with tight-fitting lid. Pack ingredients down lightly before adding another layer.

2. Cover top of jar with fabric. Attach gift tag/recipe with raffia or ribbon.

apricot-cranberry bread

1 jar Apricot-Cranberry Bread Mix

1-1/4 cups buttermilk

1/4 cup shortening

1 egg, beaten

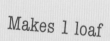

Makes 1 loaf

1. Preheat oven to 350°F. Spray 9×5-inch loaf pan with nonstick cooking spray.

2. Pour contents of jar into large bowl. Combine buttermilk, shortening and egg in small bowl until blended; stir into flour mixture just until moistened. Pour evenly into prepared pan.

3. Bake 45 to 50 minutes or until toothpick inserted into center comes out clean. Cool in pan on wire rack 10 minutes. Remove from pan; cool completely.

lentil-barley soup mix

3/4 cup dried lentils

3/4 cup pearl barley

6 vegetable bouillon cubes, unwrapped

3 tablespoons dried chopped or minced onions

2 tablespoons dried celery flakes

1 teaspoon dried minced garlic

1 teaspoon dried oregano

1 teaspoon lemon pepper

1/2 teaspoon dried rosemary

Makes
1 (1-pint) jar

1. Layer lentils and barley in 1-pint jar with tight-fitting lid. Combine remaining ingredients in resealable food storage bag. Place bag in jar.

2. Cover top of jar with fabric. Attach gift tag/recipe card with raffia or ribbon.

lentil-barley soup

1 jar Lentil-Barley Soup Mix

6 cups water

1 (28-ounce) can diced tomatoes

1 cup thinly sliced carrots

1 cup shredded Swiss cheese

Makes
8 servings

1. Place contents of jar, water and tomatoes in large saucepan. Bring to a boil over high heat. Reduce heat and simmer, covered, 45 minutes, stirring occasionally.

2. Add carrots and simmer, covered, 15 minutes more or until carrots are tender and soup thickens. Sprinkle each serving with cheese.

fruity wild rice salad mix

1/4 teaspoon curry powder

1/4 teaspoon ground cumin

1/4 teaspoon black pepper

Pinch ground red pepper

1 package (6.2 ounces) long-grain and wild rice mix (fast-cook recipe)

1/2 cup finely chopped dried apricots

1/3 cup coarsely chopped hazelnuts

2 tablespoons dehydrated chopped parsley

Makes
1 (1-pint) jar

1. Combine curry powder, cumin, black pepper and red pepper in small bowl. Pour into 1-pint wide-mouth jar with tight-fitting lid.

2. Discard rice seasoning packet or save for another recipe. Layer rice, apricots, hazelnuts and parsley attractively in jar. Pack down lightly before adding each layer. Seal jar.

3. Cover top of jar with fabric. Attach gift tag/recipe with raffia or ribbon. Attach large wooden salad fork and spoon, if desired.

Homemade gifts become extraordinary when tucked into uniquely decorated packages. Craft, stationery and kitchen supply stores carry a wide variety of supplies that can add a special touch to your gift.

fruity wild rice salad

1 jar Fruity Wild Rice Salad Mix

1-1/2 cups finely shredded or chopped red cabbage

1-1/2 tablespoons white wine vinegar

1 tablespoon honey

1/2 teaspoon salt

1-1/2 tablespoons vegetable oil

Makes
6 servings

1. Combine 1-3/4 cups water and Fruity Wild Rice Salad Mix in large saucepan. Bring to a boil. Cover and reduce heat to low. Simmer 10 to 12 minutes or until rice is tender. Remove from heat. Let stand 5 minutes.

2. Transfer to salad bowl; cool to room temperature. Stir in red cabbage.

3. Combine vinegar, honey and salt in small bowl, stirring until salt dissolves. Blend in oil. Add to salad and mix.

blueberry pancakes mix

1-1/4 cups all-purpose flour

1 tablespoon baking powder

1/2 teaspoon salt

1/4 cup light brown sugar or granulated maple sugar

1/2 cup dried blueberries

> **Makes
> 1 (1-pint) jar**

1. Combine flour, baking powder and salt in medium bowl. Pour into 1-pint wide-mouth jar with tight-fitting lid and pack down lightly. Layer brown sugar and blueberries attractively in jar. Pack down lightly before adding each layer. Seal jar.

2. Cover top of jar with fabric. Attach gift tag/recipe with raffia or ribbon. Attach large spatula, if desired.

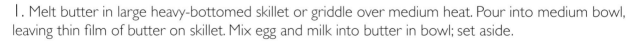

blueberry pancakes

2 tablespoons plus 2 teaspoons unsalted butter

1 egg, beaten

1-1/4 cups milk

1 jar Blueberry Pancakes Mix

Powdered sugar or maple syrup

> **Makes 10 to
> 12 pancakes**

1. Melt butter in large heavy-bottomed skillet or griddle over medium heat. Pour into medium bowl, leaving thin film of butter on skillet. Mix egg and milk into butter in bowl; set aside.

2. Pour Blueberry Pancakes Mix into large bowl; stir well. Add liquid mixture and stir to mix. *Do not beat.* Pour 1/4-cup portions of batter into skillet. Cook over medium heat 2 to 3 minutes on each side or until golden. Dust with powdered sugar.

crispy kaleidoscope eggs mix

**Makes
1 (1/2-gallon) jar**

2-1/2 cups crisp rice cereal

2 cups fruit-flavored ring-shaped cereal

3 cups mini marshmallows

1/2 cup jelly beans

1. Layer rice cereal, fruit-flavored cereal, marshmallows and jelly beans in 1/2-gallon food storage jar. Seal jar.

2. Cover top of jar with fabric. Attach gift tag/recipe with raffia or ribbon.

crispy kaleidoscope eggs

**Makes about
2 dozen eggs**

3 tablespoons butter

1 jar Crispy Kaleidoscope Eggs Mix

1. Heat butter in large microwavable bowl on HIGH 1 minute or until completely melted. Pour contents of jar into bowl. Microwave 1 minute; stir gently to combine ingredients without crushing cereal.

2. Cool 2 minutes or until easy to handle. Butter hands well and form handfuls of mixture into egg shapes about the size of real eggs. Mixture will stay moldable for 10 minutes or more.

cherry-lemon poppy seed muffins mix

2 cups all-purpose flour

1 tablespoon baking powder

1 teaspoon salt

1 cup sugar

1/2 cup dried sweet cherries, chopped

1/2 cup chopped pecans

2 tablespoons poppy seeds

Makes 1 (1-quart) jar

1. Combine flour, baking powder and salt in medium bowl. Pour into 1-quart wide-mouth jar with tight-fitting lid and pack down firmly. Add sugar and pack firmly.

2. Place cherries, pecans and poppy seeds in separate small resealable food storage bags, forcing air from bags before sealing. Place bags in jar and pack down firmly after each addition.

3. Cover top of jar with fabric. Attach gift tag/recipe with raffia or ribbon.

To keep dried fruit from sticking to your knife when chopping, coat it with nonstick cooking spray first.

cherry-lemon poppy seed muffins

1 jar Cherry-Lemon Poppy Seed Muffins Mix

3/4 cup buttermilk

1/4 cup vegetable oil

4 tablespoons unsalted butter, melted

2 eggs, lightly beaten

Grated peel from 1 lemon

1 tablespoon fresh lemon juice

2 teaspoons lemon extract

1 teaspoon vanilla

Makes 12 muffins

1. Preheat oven to 350°F. Coat 12 standard (2-1/2-inch) muffin cups with nonstick cooking spray; set aside. Remove bags from jar. Combine cherries, pecans and poppy seeds in small bowl and stir well; set aside. Place remaining contents of jar in large bowl and stir well. Make a well in center.

2. Combine buttermilk, oil, butter, eggs, lemon peel, lemon juice, lemon extract and vanilla in medium bowl. Pour into flour mixture. Stir until just blended. Stir in cherry mixture.

3. Pour batter into prepared muffin cups, filling about three-fourths full. Bake 20 to 24 minutes or until golden brown and toothpick inserted into centers comes out clean. Cool in pan 5 minutes. Transfer to wire rack to cool completely. Store in airtight container.

fudgy chocolate-amaretti brownies mix

2/3 cup unsweetened cocoa powder

1 cup all-purpose flour

1 teaspoon baking powder

1/4 teaspoon salt

1/2 cup amaretti cookie crumbs

3/4 cup granulated sugar

1/2 cup packed brown sugar

1/2 cup semisweet chocolate chips

1/3 cup powdered sugar

1. Layer all ingredients except powdered sugar in order as listed above in 1-quart food storage jar with tight-fitting lid. Lightly pack down ingredients before adding another layer. Place powdered sugar in small plastic food storage bag. Close with twist tie; cut off top of bag. Place bag in jar.

2. Cover top of jar with fabric. Attach gift tag/recipe with raffia or ribbon.

Makes
1 (1-quart) jar

fudgy chocolate-amaretti brownies

1 jar Fudgy Chocolate-Amaretti Brownies Mix

1/2 cup (1 stick) butter, softened

1 teaspoon vanilla

2 eggs

2 tablespoons almond-flavored liqueur or milk

Holiday-shaped stencil or doily with large pattern

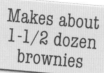

Makes about 1-1/2 dozen brownies

1. Preheat oven to 350°F. Grease 9-inch square baking pan.

2. Remove powdered sugar packet from jar. Place remaining contents of jar in large bowl; stir until well blended. Beat butter and vanilla in medium bowl with electric mixer at medium speed until smooth. Beat in eggs and liqueur. (Mixture may appear curdled.) Add butter mixture to flour mixture; stir until well blended.

3. Spoon batter into prepared pan. Press down with back of spoon. (Batter will be thick and sticky. It will spread out during baking.) Bake 20 to 25 minutes or until brownies spring back when lightly touched. *Do not overbake.* Cool in pan on wire rack.

4. Before serving, place stencil on top of brownies. Dust with powdered sugar; remove stencil. Cut into bars.

toffee delight muffins mix

3 cups all-purpose flour

2/3 cup packed brown sugar

1 package (8 ounces) toffee baking bits

1 tablespoon baking powder

1 teaspoon baking soda

1/2 teaspoon salt

Makes 1 (1-quart) jar

1. Layer ingredients attractively in any order in 1-quart food storage jar with tight-fitting lid. Pack ingredients down firmly before adding another layer.

2. Cover top of jar with fabric. Attach gift tag/recipe with raffia or ribbon.

toffee delight muffins

1 jar Toffee Delight Muffins Mix

1 cup milk

1 cup sour cream

6 tablespoons butter, melted

2 eggs

2 teaspoons vanilla

Makes 24 muffins

1. Preheat oven to 400°F. Grease or paper-line 24 standard (2-1/2-inch) muffin cups.

2. Pour contents of jar into large bowl. Combine milk, sour cream, butter, eggs and vanilla in medium bowl until blended; stir into flour mixture just until moistened. Spoon evenly into prepared muffin cups, filling two-thirds full.

3. Bake 16 to 18 minutes or until toothpick inserted into centers comes out clean. Remove from pans; cool on wire racks 10 minutes. Serve warm or cool completely.

gifts from a Jar

window-to-my-heart cookies mix

2-1/4 cups flour

1/2 teaspoon salt

1/4 teaspoon baking powder

1/4 cup packed brown sugar

1 cup dried sweetened cranberries, chopped

1/2 cup powdered sugar

15 to 20 cherry-flavored or cinnamon-flavored hard candies

Makes
1 (1-quart) jar

1. Combine flour, salt and baking powder in medium bowl. Layer flour mixture, brown sugar, cranberries and powdered sugar in 1-quart food storage jar with tight-fitting lid. Pack ingredients down lightly before adding each layer. Place candies in small resealable food storage bag; seal and place on top. Seal jar.

2. Cover top of jar with fabric. Attach gift tag/recipe with raffia or ribbon.

window-to-my-heart cookies

1 jar Window-to-My-Heart Cookies Mix

1 cup (2 sticks) plus 2 tablespoons butter, softened

1 teaspoon vanilla

Makes about
3 dozen cookies

1. Remove candies from jar. Crush candies in bag into fine crumbs with rolling pin or mallet; set aside. Beat butter and vanilla in large bowl with electric mixer at medium speed. Gradually beat in remaining contents of jar. Wrap dough and refrigerate 30 minutes.

2. Preheat oven to 325°F. Roll dough out on floured surface to 1/4-inch thickness. Cut into heart-shaped cookies with large cookie cutter. Cut out center of each cookie with small heart-shaped cookie cutter.

3. Transfer cookies to cookie sheets lined with foil. Sprinkle thin layer of crushed candy into empty centers. Bake 20 minutes or until edges are light brown and candy is melted. Cool on cookie sheets until candy centers are firm.

home-style chicken & rice soup mix

1/2 cup dried yellow split peas or wild rice

2 tablespoons dried minced onion

2 tablespoons dried vegetable flakes, soup greens or dehydrated vegetables

2 teaspoons chicken bouillon granules

1 teaspoon dried thyme

1/2 teaspoon dried minced garlic

1/2 teaspoon dried marjoram

1/2 teaspoon lemon pepper

1 cup uncooked brown rice

1 bay leaf

Makes
1 (1-pint) jar

1. Layer split peas, onion, vegetable flakes, bouillon granules, thyme, garlic, marjoram, lemon pepper and rice in 1-pint food storage jar with tight-fitting lid. Slide bay leaf down side of jar. Seal jar.

2. Cover top of jar with fabric. Attach gift tag/recipe with raffia or ribbon.

Note: Dried vegetable flakes and soup greens are available in the spice section of large supermarkets. Also, look for dried vegetable flakes (bell peppers, carrots, etc.) in the bulk food section of specialty food markets such as natural food stores.

Assemble a beautiful gift basket with a jar of Home-Style Chicken & Rice Soup Mix, a can of tomato sauce and corn muffin mix. Complete the basket with decorative soup bowls.

home-style chicken & rice soup

1 jar Home-Style Chicken & Rice Soup Mix

6 to 7 cups water

1 can (8 ounces) tomato sauce

2 cups cubed cooked chicken

Salt and black pepper

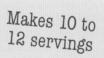

Makes 10 to 12 servings

1. Combine contents of jar, water and tomato sauce in Dutch oven. Bring to a boil over high heat. Cover; reduce heat and simmer 1 hour or until peas are tender.

2. Stir in chicken. Cook over low heat 10 to 15 minutes or until chicken is heated through. Remove and discard bay leaf. Season to taste with salt and pepper.

spiced-up cocoa mix

1 cup sugar

1/2 cup unsweetened cocoa powder

1 tablespoon all-purpose flour

2 teaspoons ground cinnamon

1-1/2 teaspoons ground cloves

1/2 teaspoon salt

1/2 teaspoon chili powder

1/4 teaspoon ground allspice

Mini marshmallows

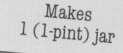

Makes
1 (1-pint) jar

1. Whisk together all ingredients except marshmallows in small bowl. Place mixture in 1-pint jar with tight-fitting lid. Place marshmallows in resealable food storage bag; place bag in jar. (Add or remove marshmallows as space allows.)

2. Cover top of jar with fabric. Attach gift tag/recipe with raffia or ribbon.

spiced-up cocoa

1/3 cup water

3/4 cup Spiced-Up Cocoa Mix

4 cups milk

3/4 teaspoon vanilla

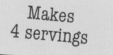

Makes
4 servings

1. Set aside mini marshmallows. Bring water to a boil in medium saucepan over high heat. Whisk Spiced-Up Cocoa Mix into boiling water, stirring constantly. Reduce heat to medium; cook and stir 1 to 2 minutes or until thick and smooth.

2. Add milk and vanilla; heat to steaming (not boiling), stirring constantly. Pour cocoa into 4 mugs and top with mini marshmallows. Serve hot.

The publisher would like to thank the companies and organizations listed below for the use of their recipes and photographs in this publication.

Campbell Soup Company

Cream of Wheat® Cereal

Dole Food Company, Inc.

EAGLE BRAND®

Fleischmann's® Margarines and Spreads

The Hershey Company

©2009 Kraft Foods, KRAFT, KRAFT Hexagon Logo,
PHILADELPHIA AND PHILADELPHIA Logo are
registered trademarks of Kraft Foods Holdings, Inc. All rights reserved.

© Mars, Incorporated 2009

Mott's® is a registered trademark of Mott's, LLP

Nestlé USA

Ortega®, A Division of B&G Foods, Inc.

Watkins Incorporated

VOLUME MEASUREMENTS (dry)

$^1/_8$ teaspoon = 0.5 mL
$^1/_4$ teaspoon = 1 mL
$^1/_2$ teaspoon = 2 mL
$^3/_4$ teaspoon = 4 mL
1 teaspoon = 5 mL
1 tablespoon = 15 mL
2 tablespoons = 30 mL
$^1/_4$ cup = 60 mL
$^1/_3$ cup = 75 mL
$^1/_2$ cup = 125 mL
$^2/_3$ cup = 150 mL
$^3/_4$ cup = 175 mL
1 cup = 250 mL
2 cups = 1 pint = 500 mL
3 cups = 750 mL
4 cups = 1 quart = 1 L

VOLUME MEASUREMENTS (fluid)

1 fluid ounce (2 tablespoons) = 30 mL
4 fluid ounces ($^1/_2$ cup) = 125 mL
8 fluid ounces (1 cup) = 250 mL
12 fluid ounces (1$^1/_2$ cups) = 375 mL
16 fluid ounces (2 cups) = 500 mL

WEIGHTS (mass)

$^1/_2$ ounce = 15 g
1 ounce = 30 g
3 ounces = 90 g
4 ounces = 120 g
8 ounces = 225 g
10 ounces = 285 g
12 ounces = 360 g
16 ounces = 1 pound = 450 g

DIMENSIONS

$^1/_{16}$ inch = 2 mm
$^1/_8$ inch = 3 mm
$^1/_4$ inch = 6 mm
$^1/_2$ inch = 1.5 cm
$^3/_4$ inch = 2 cm
1 inch = 2.5 cm

OVEN TEMPERATURES

250°F = 120°C
275°F = 140°C
300°F = 150°C
325°F = 160°C
350°F = 180°C
375°F = 190°C
400°F = 200°C
425°F = 220°C
450°F = 230°C

BAKING PAN SIZES

Utensil	Size in Inches/Quarts	Metric Volume	Size in Centimeters
Baking or Cake Pan (square or rectangular)	8×8×2	2 L	20×20×5
	9×9×2	2.5 L	23×23×5
	12×8×2	3 L	30×20×5
	13×9×2	3.5 L	33×23×5
Loaf Pan	8×4×3	1.5 L	20×10×7
	9×5×3	2 L	23×13×7
Round Layer Cake Pan	8×1½	1.2 L	20×4
	9×1½	1.5 L	23×4
Pie Plate	8×1¼	750 mL	20×3
	9×1¼	1 L	23×3
Baking Dish or Casserole	1 quart	1 L	—
	1½ quart	1.5 L	—
	2 quart	2 L	—